Books are to be returned on or before
the last date below.

5 MAR 1996 A

12 MAR 1996 A

28 SEP 1999

30 SEP 1996

6 OCT 1999

16 FEB 1998 A

18 SEP 1998 A

- 7 MAR 2000

14 MAR 2000

- 5 FEB 2001

28 NOV 2001

A

26 NOV 1998

LIBREX —

15 FEB 1999

The Author

Authors' biographies appear in books for several reasons: the publishers need something to fill the dust jacket on a hard cover book; the publishers know from bitter experience that the author in question seldom writes to the planned length; the author is vain; or, the most respectable reason, readers may have more respect for the contents when they can identify some authority in the author's experience. We shall concentrate on the latter.

John Courtis is professionally an unusual combination, a chartered accountant and member of the IPM. His work experience since qualifying as an accountant in 1959 has been largely in management selection, but he also spent three years in the RAF, five years on the finance staff of Ford Motor Company and, most recently, seven years as Chairman of a client manufacturing PLC.

He has been active in management education for the Institute of Chartered Accountants and others, served as Chairman of the recruitment sector trade association (the Federation of Recruitment and Employment Services), and has written numerous books on management subjects, from *Cost Effective Recruitment, Money Matters for Managers* and *Interviews: skills and strategy* for the IPM, through *Communicating for Results* and *Managing by Mistake* for the Institute of Chartered Accountants, *Marketing Services* and *Selling Yourself in the Management Market* for the British Institute of Management down to *Bluffers Guides* on *Accountancy, Management* and *Photography* for Oval Projects.

All of this is useful background. The relevant foreground is that he has spent over twenty years in the recruitment trade, most of it as head of John Courtis and Partners.

Fortunately his leisure interests have absolutely no relevance to the subject. He is no longer a member of Mensa and is physically unfit for most sporting activities.

Recruiting for Profit

John Courtis

Cartoons by Joe Stockton

Institute of Personnel Management

First published 1989

Phototypeset by James Jenkins Typesetting (Wandsworth)
and printed in Great Britain by
Short Run Press Ltd, Exeter, Devon.

British Library Cataloguing in Publication Data
Courtis, John
Recruiting for profit.
   1. Personnel management
   I. Title   II. Institute of Personnel Management 658.3.

ISBN 0-85292-427-5

Contents

*Good practice is not an end in
itself – it must address the
corporate objectives*

'Certainly we don't practise discrimination, but
this *is* a monastery'

Foreword

Should you read this book? And if so, why? It is intended for several categories of people, not just professional recruiters (although even they may find something to interest or amuse them):

- personnel practitioners who want a tool with which to persuade or educate their colleagues
- all other functional managers who recruit
- general managers who want to improve their teams
- students
- people who liked one of the author's other books and hope that this one may be equally painless.

The objectives. In brief, there are several routes to profit. Lower costs, higher revenues, better margins and better return on capital employed. This book explores all of these.

The context. Where are we starting from? The author, with a background of thirty-five years in business (he started very young), knows that mediocre practice in recruitment is the norm. Just dragging corporate standards up to a no-fault minimum can work wonders. Ways to do even better appear within.

The contents. This book is not an absolute guide, not wholly original, not overly comprehensive. In particular it is complementary to *Interviews: skills and strategy* from the same author and publisher. Other good books will be mentioned. So will examples close to you. But this text may suggest new ways of considering and applying old lessons. And its lighter side may help you to present good practice to colleagues previously immune to good practice or employment law in the twentieth century. There are also cogent arguments for hiring minority groups against whom your colleages remain deeply prejudiced (not for themselves, of course, but for their colleagues . . .).

Businesses run on people and money.
You have to recruit the people well
to recruit the money well.

'I know Hornblower's ex-Navy, but would
you trust his recruits?'

Introduction

This book is dedicated to the concept that recruitment, too often treated as a necessary evil, can be and ought to be a positive force – one of the most significant for any organization.

Most organizations exist on two key resources, money and people. The people are vital if you are to apply the money and what it buys, so recruitment is not an evil, and in some cases may not be necessary either.

The ultimate objective of a business is likely to be profit, with survival but not necessarily growth, implied, The same principle applies to its people. Getting bigger and hiring more people must not become an objective unless this genuinely furthers the *ultimate* objective.

Making more profits with the same resources and effort may be better than growing to an unwieldy size. Making the same profits with less resources and effort is also sound. Making more profits with less resources and effort is even better. The message is *quality* rather than quantity. And it applies to employment levels and therefore to recruitment. For those of you in non-profit-making organizations this message is even more important. The organization has to provide its services without a profit-making machine to justify or to permit growth. Efficient use of all resources is, therefore, crucial.

Recruiting the right resources in the first place is a precondition. Even those who train brilliantly have to have something to work on.

Before we explore the positive contribution good recruitment can make, it is important that the difference between good and bad is clearly understood. It is not generally appreciated, even by some experienced recruiters, how wide is the gap between good and bad practice – nor the likely consequences.

A few basic examples may help:

Good	Bad
• a job specification exists	it does not
• it correctly identifies ideal and minimum requirements	imprecise or idealistic candidate definition

1

Good	Bad
• salary correctly assessed, with any flexibility stated	salary unclear or inadequate; flexibility undeclared or non-existent
• advertisement gives adequate information with warm reply instructions	ad copy is unclear, with poor disclosure and unsympathetic reply instructions
• the medium is right	medium irrelevant or in-adequate
• interviews quickly follow candidates' response	delay loses candidates
• good interview	counter-productive interview which demotivates candidates or rejects good ones
• prompt follow-up	more delays
• well-researched offer to right candidate	inadequate offer *or* adequate offer to bad candidate

There are many other problems and the horrid consequences will be explored further, but the constructive benefits of getting recruitment right will also be covered. Most organizations are recruiting most of the time. If they can do everything a little bit better the benefits include:

- less time and money spent on recruitment
- more scarce recruits per pound
- quicker results from the recruitment process
- reduced employee turnover
- same results with less people
- better profits from better people
- replacement for sub-standard people
- loyal people, nicer team-mates, developable people
- square pegs for square holes
- penalty costs of bad practice avoided or contained.

All being well, much of the book should appear commonsense. It is intended to be a menu of 'thought-starters' and in this area one new idea or a half-forgotten one remembered can save thousands of pounds, or make tens of thousands eventually.

Someone near you is in the wrong job or the wrong organization. Better recruitment might have prevented this.

PRELIMINARIES

The Status Quo

This book is being written as the 1990s loom ahead: the IPM has been in existence for over 75 years, yet most organizations in the UK are using recruitment practices which were unsatisfactory half a century ago.

Several commentators have expressed disquiet about specific defects in the recruitment process but seem to be apathetic about the wider implications. Nobody I know has sat down with a clean sheet of paper and listed the full range of problems and attitudes which combine to make recruitment in the UK so mediocre. Here goes!

The author knows of no organization which does not suffer from one or more of the following problems:

(a) some recruitment is perceived as just a necessary nuisance

(b) little or no research has been done to identify the ideal and the minimum criteria for successful performance in key jobs, except perhaps in some skilled trades

(c) recruitment is the automatic reaction to some or all employee departures, regardless of corporate circumstances

(d) the candidate specification is usually an arbitrary list, made without obvious link to past job performance, by people who have little or no knowledge of the syllabus in any of the educational or professional qualifications they are specifying as necessary ingredients

(e) subjective judgements at interviews are the prime filter – usually the only one

(f) most recruiters look for ways to reject people rather than ways they could be used by their organization

(g) objective judgements, through tests of any kind, are not fully utilized or are wholly absent

(h) employee turnover is inexplicably high in some areas and there are perceived skills shortages in key areas

(i) poor practice is self-perpetuating because bad recruitment produces bad managers and bad managers tend to recruit badly

(j) very few companies have a post-audit system and there is little incentive to volunteer clear disclosure of a failed hiring

(k) employers often tell people what was expected of them and where they fell short only when formally warning them, or firing them: 'There was no time to put this in writing or put it to the victims in any way before because everyone was so busy . . .'

(l) it is necessary to hire experienced people, at great expense, because there is no time, no money or nobody available to train them

(m) as a consequence, you buy other companies' irrelevant and sometimes bad experience, at a premium wage

(n) people get hired because they are personable and handsome

(o) people get hired because they are not a threat to their (insecure) bosses

(p) most managers believe their judgements at interview are objective and have a bearing on future job performance

(q) few companies have trained their managers to interview well, or at all

(r) few companies have trained their managers to interpret test results

(s) where interviews and objective test results conflict, the subjective, unvalidated interview result is usually preferred – or any negative points, from either, take precedence in the decision!

(t) members of professional bodies are admitted entirely on the basis of examinations which ignore their suitability for the mainstream work of the profession, in terms of aptitude, interest or psychological make-up: consequently their 'qualifications' do not fit them for later jobs – or management.

In some ways this is reassuring. The norm is so unsatisfactory at the moment that almost every aspect of current recruitment practice is capable of improvement. The potential benefits are massive. However, enough of the bad. My basic management philosophy is to favour constructive action rather than look backwards, or sideways, at those things which deserve criticism. Avoiding gratuitous error is all very well, but we have to do better than that. You can.

We have, furthermore, a powerful incentive if we wish to remain in control of our recruitment. Candidates are not operating in a vacuum. They are aware, or may become aware, of the defects in the recruitment process and take advantage of them.

Two adverse consequences may well result. The first is that a good candidate may take advantage of the defects and be hired for a job he or she wants which doesn't turn out as described. The result is an unhappy hiring. The second is that an unsatisfactory candidate may get through by cheating or role-playing. The candidate may be happy but the employer may not.

There is one consolation. A good candidate may also cheat the system to be hired into an appropriate job. However, it seems unwise to rely on this happening often, or at all. And will they work well with the rest of the hirings who, on the above showing, may be misfits?

Candidates may become aware of the defects in
the recruitment process . . .

The True Cost of Recruitment

It is not widely understood why professional recruiters get so deeply depressed about the state of recruitment in the UK. Pleas for best practice, or any suggestion that we should drag management recruitment up to the standards applied nowadays in selecting support employees (anything from skilled trades to publicans) fall on deaf ears because the downside risk is not fully appreciated.

First, let us consider the sort of person you might hope to recruit before we discuss the horrible alternative.

The ideal for which you are looking might well be summarized like this:

- adult, assertive and well balanced
- gives colleagues credit for commonsense
- operates 'no surprises' style
- does things in good time or you know why it is not being done
- communicates clearly and openly
- boringly reliable: always on time; good time management
- unselfish, aware of others' feelings
- develops people well and is well respected
- decisive and confident
- thinks well: good problem analyst
- listens: remembers
- apolitical: straightforward
- analyses errors to avoid repetition: always constructive (but doesn't blame people).
- trustworthy: honours undertakings
- clear perception of errors: not afraid to acknowledge mistakes
- hires well, so firing is seldom necessary
- social life subordinated to work obligations (within reason)
- fluent speaker and writer: persuasive
- not threatened by excellence around him/her
- supportive, warm, encouraging to subordinates

- authoritative and powerful
- doesn't let prejudices interfere with judgement
- intelligent: applies intelligence well: open mind
- constantly improves practice of own department.

These paragons are rare, but when they can be found, the benefit is not just being better than average; there are headcount savings because they don't need to be monitored or supervised. Failure to recruit properly brings a major downside risk. Consider the alternative.

The following profile is of a real manager, now in charge of a significant profit centre. He or she represents a managerial 'time bomb', as follows:

Assumes the worst of colleagues
Bears grudges and fuels them
Conceals bad news, hoping for miracles
Delays beyond most deadlines
Equivocates or lies when on the defensive
Forgets key meetings or their location
Greedy, spoiled and self-centred
Harasses subordinates rather than trains them
Indecisive and insecure
Justifies by assumptions rather than facts
Knocks others' initiatives
Listens badly; prefers to talk
Manipulative and devious
Needs to blame people
Own errors not recognized
Promises are broken or bent
Quite remarkable capacity for self-deception
Rationalizes firing rather than curing people
Social life interferes with work
Tenuous grasp of business English
Undermines subordinates who are brighter or better . . .
Vindictive
Weak
Xenophobic

These characteristics are relatively unlikely to be detected by employers *or* potential employees at interview. There isn't a lot potential employees can do, apart from consulting people who

. . . bears grudges and fuels them

have left the organization, but employers, using references properly, formal tests or even work samples, have a better chance.

For those recruiters who think they are equal to the challenge, this person (and others similar) will be on the market this year, but they will not be too easy to recognize at interview because initially they will be perceived as:

- good looking
- above medium height
- charming
- ageless
- having a sense of humour
- well dressed
- vivacious
- articulate
- sincere
- well versed in management theory
- graduates
- mildly sporting
- caring parents
- having impeccable track records

All those of you who are skilled interviewers will of course have a chance to detect the Hyde beneath, but someone else is going to hire him or her . . .

This may seem an over-dramatic way to make the point, but the point is very important. The tacit assumption about bad recruitment is that it produces employees who are less good than you might wish.

This presupposes that employees are measured on a scale from 100 per cent excellent to zero, with zero being a wholly neutral contribution. A moment's thought about any organization you know will bring to mind someone whose behaviour is in some respects bad or negative and detracts from their own contribution or from others'. Mathematicians will be aware of the need to have negative values on a graph. You need them on a management grid too! But you don't need them on your team, unless *massively* outweighed by their positive values.

Skilled interviewers will detect the Hyde beneath . . .

Driving in Fog

There is another problem of which you need to be aware. The author suspects that there may be something hallucinogenic about the recruitment process which causes otherwise reasonable people to lose their grasp on reality. In no other management activity are managers so willing to be gratuitously encumbered with error and omission, often of their own making.

For instance, if dealing with money, it is generally accepted that if interest is to be earned on it, certain rules have to be followed: it is has be delivered, on time, to a reputable organization which will undertake to pay interest for the required term, subject to agreed notice of withdrawal. Further, if the interest is to be paid gross rather than net, certain statutory conditions have to be met and the deposit-taking organization has to be chosen with your organization's status and this need in mind. Managers accept that these rules are implacable and that any omission or breach will result in the loss of some part of the interest earned. They do not expect banks and building societies to make gracious gestures to bridge gaps created by the depositor's omissions.

Alas, when the return sought on their resources represents successful recruitment, a lunatic attitude overtakes them: the basic rules which govern good recruitment are flouted, with a cavalier disregard for the consequences. The hallucinogenic analogy was carefully chosen, for they enter a fantasy world in which, high on corporate vanity, they behave as if candidates are not real people, just a vast admiring throng clamouring to be hired by the organization which, for the sake of brevity, we shall call Dudco Ltd. Dudco executives recruit in blinkers. They not only ignore the basic rules outlined elsewhere in this book, they also gild the lily with certain specialized examples of self-delusion.

They believe, for instance, that:

- it is not necessary to apply marketing philosophy to Dudco recruitment, because everyone relevant in the country knows about the company and the best of those are keen to work for Dudco at an unexciting salary in a particularly inconvenient and desolate part of a generally unpleasant urban sprawl

- there is a buyers' market and Dudco is the buyer. In spite of the fact that competitors keep complaining about skills shortages

- bad advertising is a useful test of candidates' interest, determination and general willingness to fight their way in to the Dudco ranks: delay, indecision, poor communication, stress interviews and broken promises are all useful tools in this test programme.

For these and related reasons, all the Dudcos will get the people they deserve. You can do better, not least because the Dudco attitudes are widespread and if you avoid them your recruitment profile looks dramatically better by comparison. In ways which good candidates will notice and respond to. In particular, you will then have the right to be selective and will have a reasonable selection of relevant people from whom to select. Dudco, by contrast, sets high standards initially and then, when malpractice and delay have left them with a poor choice, will panic and indiscriminately lower their criteria.

Dudco attitudes abound. Make sure there isn't a Dudco-trained manager quietly applying these principles somewhere in your corporate structure.

Delay is probably the easiest Dudco symptom to spot. The 'good types will wait for Dudco' theory is rampant regardless of the fact that the only candidates who can afford to wait are those who are not attracting offers from other companies.

Even if there are good guys (Dudco prefers men, preferably able-bodied, white and heterosexual) who are prepared to wait; when they get a sensible offer from another group the 'bird in hand' theory applies and even several hypothetical, future offers from several Dudcos in the bush cannot compete with a prompt real offer. This is particularly so because Dudco offers, when they finally emerge, tend to be pitched at such a mean level that they do not justify changing companies. The low offers result sometimes because Dudco has failed to quantify the candidate's existing package, sometimes because Dudco believes people move for love rather than money (parity with the old package, or less, is not unusual in a Dudco offer) and sometimes because the offer letter omits the second page which lists all the worthwhile fringe benefits . . .

However, delay is the most visible symptom. Watch for it.

All DUDCOS will get the people they deserve

Footnote

Dudco, by the way, is not just a creature of the author's fevered imagination. It is an amalgam of three fairly well-known PLCs, one in financial services, one in retail and the third in manufacturing and marketing. Between them they *each* achieve at least 60 per cent of the faults quoted in an average year – quite apart from the recruitment which is unknown to the author.

Candidate Power

The preceding section may have given you a negative impression. There is worse to come before we get on to the positive bits. Candidates have become more demanding. Recruitment is now much more user-driven than it used to be and second-rate recruitment practice brings its own deserts. In brief, you are going to be judged by the quality of your recruitment and the better candidates will take a cool look at recruitment omissions and malpractice and decide that they are a symptom of corporate mediocrity.

The lesson is basic: avoid gratuitous error. Adding excellence, flair, creative genius and inventive advertising copy is all very well but if other parts of the process do not drag themselves up to the acceptable minimum, you might as well tear up the ads and start again.

It is rather like cross-country driving. Planning routes and tactics which will permit you to average fifty miles per hour rather than forty gains you more time, and is less effort than doing sixty miles per hour. In recruitment you also have co-drivers who will drag your average down. Plan for them too if you want the recruitment journey to be smooth and above average. It is no use arranging that your bit of the route averages a mile a minute if the co-driver gets lost, has to stop too often, runs out of fuel or leaves the car to make an unscheduled deviation. The people who are expecting you may not wait. Candidates are the same.

Finally, if at any point in the following pages you observe a maudlin or plaintive note creep into the author's observations, please remember that he has, for over twenty years, been feeling like a racehorse in tandem with a carthorse or, in certain cases, like a reliable carthorse in the shafts with a racehorse, while the latter is pointing in a different direction . . .! Candidates are not the only ones with feelings.

Would you let a bricklayer mend your computer? Then why trust accountants, engineers, computer experts and sales staff to play with selection matters?

Accentuate the Positive

The emphasis so far has been on somewhat negative things like the practical disadvantages of failure and the cost of failure. You will be relieved to learn that the rest of the book falls naturally into three sections – mostly constructive.

The first covers ways you can make recruitment more cost-effective, both by doing the same things cheaper or better things at the same or lower cost. The second is about the way recruitment can make the organization more efficient and/or profitable. The third includes the afterthoughts – best practice which will not necessarily pay instant dividends, but must be right eventually!

This area, of best practice, presents a couple of problems which had better be addressed now, lest your adverse reaction prevents you from considering examples impartially. Best practice is not an end in itself. It is not a valid objective. It is justified only when it serves the organization's objectives or it is a no-cost alternative to practices less than best or, in many cases, worse than average. This is not an argument for bad practice, merely a recognition that the end, the corporate objective, is more important than the means. Note the careful phraseology. It does not automatically justify any means, but it is more important than your precise *choice* of means. It follows that if your colleagues, or competitors, can point to successful results from imperfect practice you will need more than a slogan about best practice to convince them of the error (or omission) of their ways.

This brings us to the second problem: justifying best practice to malpractitioners may not be easy and, in some cases, may not be feasible. Nevertheless, it is always important to attempt justification. Saying 'This is the way to do it' offers no incentive to someone who knows that, on the contrary, *'That* is the way to do it, the way we've always done it'. Just a little leverage may help. It is rather like advertising, you can employ fear, greed or even sex. You must identify the adverse consequences of the present practice or the favourable consequences of better practice.

This is a simple communication exercise. The progression of persuasion goes something like this:

KEEP OFF THE GRASS

PLEASE KEEP OFF THE GRASS

Please keep off the grass because it is newly seeded

Please keep off the grass, there's a nicer route here

KEEP OFF THE GRASS: FINE £50

QUICKSAND!

NUDIST BEACH *THIS* WAY!

Not all these could be, or should be, translated into personnel practice but it is useful to remember their existence. In particular, the three key points which are (for those of you still trying to figure out the recruitment equivalent of a nudist beach):

- saying please, or at least couching your requests politely
- providing a 'because' which has some credibility
- offering a threat or incentive which goes beyond the mere logic of the 'because' item

It must be stressed that the threats and/or incentives are additional to the reason why, not substitutional, and should only be used when the matter cannot be resolved by the reason why, presented nicely.

Very few people actively want to be bad. Most problems arise because they perceive their acts and omissions as acceptable or even good. If they can be convinced otherwise, some of the problems may vanish.

The difficulty about educating them is that everyone around the culprits has a very clear perception of what is 'wrong' and 'right'. Unfortunately the shades of grey are infinite and your perception differs in some respect from everyone else's. Don't assume. Communicate positively and a common standard will emerge. It may not be perfect but at least it will be standard and better than what went before. But it has to be supported by the reasons why. People are stubborn and, whether stupid or bright, need some justification for changing their practices. After all they were doing it wrong for reasons which they regarded as very acceptable! You have to overcome those reasons with better ones.

The process of persuasion

Is Your Vacancy Really Necessary?

Before you specify the vacancy and the likely candidates, it is always important to ask whether there really *is* a vacancy. Most employers believe that they do this, but the enquiry is often superficial. Asking more thoroughly, in different ways, is one of the most efficient ways of cutting your costs at a stroke. The questions depend, to some extent, on the nature of your perceived need and indeed the nature of your organization, but should normally include some of the following:

- is it really a full-time job?
- is it full-time all year round?
- could it be done by job-sharers?
- could it be done part-time with better computer support, or some other aid?
- could those N jobs be done by N − 1 people of a slightly different specification than the current or past mix?
- does the market-place still have a supply of permanent employees willing to do this work or is it, for example, a temps/contract monopoly? If so, can we take advantage of this flexibility?
- could it be done by outworkers: perhaps by the employee who is retiring from the post?
- when did we last consider whether the work practices around this job could be improved so as to eliminate or reduce it?
- do the benefits from the performance of this job appreciably exceed the true cost of filling it? And is that margin really enough, having considered indirect expenses such as space?

There will be other questions unique to your own environment. Make sure that they are asked and satisfactorily answered. Supervisors and managers tend to be superficial about this matter. They seldom recognize that every extra employee needing supervision reduces the time available for managing the business. They also forget, when short-staffed, that more time spent on training might enable N − 1 to do the work of N.

It may seem odd that someone in the recruitment business should argue for headcount savings but, both as a consultant and as a small employer, the author knows how much unnecessary people cost.

The most significant example which comes to mind is a financial adviser who makes a big thing about the fact that he comes to the customers and only charges them for his time when he is on site, wholly available to them. This is a very attractive argument to people who have had bills for thousands of pounds from professional practices who do not appear to have been in touch or, indeed, done anything since the previous bill.

However, although his services may well be a bargain (so may those of the absentee advisers, but they have a PR problem) we observe that his own premises do not have to be big enough to accommodate him and his equivalents all the time. Nor do they need to be in a fashionable bit of central London.

Better still, from his point of view, the customers are bearing all or part of the following direct or indirect costs and expenses:

- *space* – rent, rates, upkeep, depreciation, heat, light, water, consumable stores, cleaning, security, etc
- *support* – wages, NIC, pension, fringe benefits, bonuses, space as above and peripheral costs as below
- *communication* – telephone, fax, telex, photocopying, word-processor, typewriter – plus their depreciation – rentals, leases, stationery, electricity, maintenance, interest on capital employed, travel expenses and so on
- *idle time* – even our subject, the adviser, has some of this; so do his and your support staff. They drink tea, telephone friends, answer calls of nature and, in his case, calls from other clients.

The lesson is basic. If you can avoid employing one supervisor or manager you also avoid paying for all or part of an assistant (whether you call him/her a secretary, PA, deputy or dogsbody doesn't matter – managers tend to need somebody to delegate to) *and* all the costs implied above.

If you take into account the true costs of modern city-centre space, one unnecessary manager with support may be costing not just say a salary of £25,000, but more than £100,000 per annum.

Bring on the Clones

There is an old theory that bosses should not be allowed to recruit unaided, for fear that they will recruit in their own image. This has been tacitly accepted for far too long, because it is partially right, but that acceptance blinds us to two different problems and their related opportunities.

In the first place, bosses generally make very different errors. They recruit people who are nice, personable, non-threatening, safe or not bright enough. There are many more possibilities – most of which spell trouble – but recruiting replicas is not a major problem. The only reason we can say the theory is partially right is that bosses recruit *non-replicas* (superficially similar) with those backgrounds with which they are comfortable. Hence the public-school Oxbridge male with an Army past who still plays cricket may empathize with similar products, but they are seldom replicas.

In the second place, recruiting people with the key character-istics of existing good performers, whether bosses or supporters, would be a very good thing. Unfortunately, most companies don't do this because they lack objective information about the key criteria and sometimes don't really know who the best performers really are.

Both problems are soluble and the potential benefits are massive, but the solutions require some effort and a commitment to change, from all the managers involved. They also require you to choose some objective measurement of the people involved, once you have properly identified those whose operational performance best addresses corporate or local objectives. This identification is crucial, but beyond the scope of this section. Instead, let us focus on the review of a sample group, the future employees and, most important, under-recognized existing employees whom you may be able to redirect into more suitable jobs as a result of such a programme.

The sample review is important. The only comment I can use-fully make about identifying the sample is that you should take a second opinion about your criteria from someone professionally qualified. The amateur criteria which are normally identified may be subjective and irrelevant. Only when you have objective criteria can you pick your sample and your later tests. For instance, to take a crude example, the best sales rep may not be the one whose order book is largest. Others may be better at tending difficult patches or doing things which bring in orders for other people, or create new customers elsewhere in the organization. Alternatively, in backroom functions those who appear to work hardest may not be the most effective. Take a second opinion about your criteria from someone less involved than yourself and from the tester whom you are to use.

In particular, do ensure that the characteristics required in lower level jobs are not included in the criteria necessary for the managerial jobs above. In a company which has traditionally promoted the best sales reps to be managers, the good managerial sample you use as a base may well have these characteristics, but the coincidence may arise from past bias, not because of any real need. Similarly, in a traditional environment obsessed with turnover, the sales rep who concentrates on producing sales at good margins rather than maximizing turnover may not automatically be identified, yet he or she may well be demonstrating the greatest capacity for advancement.

It would be presumptuous to suggest a perfect package for all situations but the characteristics you may want to test will probably include:

- intelligence
- team behaviour
- personality factors
- interests
- aptitudes
- practical skills.

The encouraging thing about this list is that, among the several thousand tests now available in the English language, there are many tests which will provide you with relatively painless assessments on any or all of these characteristics. We will cover tests in slightly more depth later, but do note that you have a choice and that administering these tests can take minutes rather than hours and in many cases simple scores can be generated quickly (or instantaneously if you select those for which software is available).

25

The Infernal Triangle

If you accept the theory about cloning you will later need to consider tests and related specifications. Even if you don't accept the test argument, good candidate specifications are an essential pre-condition for good recruitment, and will need careful consideration.

Most specifications are incomplete. They list the ideal candidate's virtues and fail to identify the minimum; or they list candidate specifications not available at the quoted rewards; or they manage to list rewards and specifications which match but do not address the candidates' willingness to consider the job in question. The three *must* match. Unless all three sides of the triangle link up you might as well not start the exercise.

For instance, if the rewards do not match the candidate specification nobody relevant will reply. If the rewards and specification match but the job is out of line in one direction or another the candidates will fall out before accepting the job or, worse, shortly after joining.

Finally, if there is synergy between the specification and job and specification and rewards, but the rewards are out of line with the job, you have probably wrongly specified the candidate and you will get lots of replies but the rewards/candidate mix will be qualitatively incompatible.

In many cases the major service we do for clients is to force them to get the triangle right before we start work. Once this relationship has been rationalized many subsequent problems are eliminated.

The difficulty is not that the recruitment exercise will fail: this is a symptom which permits you to cure the problem, albeit with some delay and expense. The greater problem is that you may recruit (or get very close to it) without realizing that the mismatch is going to make you hire someone too good or too weak for the job.

Either can be disastrous. Paying too much is worse than paying too little, because it increases the chance that you will hire unsuccessfully. Overspecifying is self-defeating, so failure will force you back to a more sensible specification. Similarly, linking a demanding job to a weak candidate specification will, all being well, have you interviewing people who are patently too weak for the post, so you are saved by the bell.

Incidentally, this is where we get into one of the more sensitive areas as regards age. Employers who want a bright, young, developable professional will often specify a salary package which is more than the immediate job needs, but will buy them excellence for their future development plans. Older, and arguably more pedestrian, candidates who could do the job well, apply and are rejected. Sometimes this is right – if the development need is paramount – but on many occasions the immediate job is the primary problem and the development element is a faint gleam in the corporate eye. Being clear in advance about the balance between these two can produce better shortlists, more cheaply or more easily.

The general problem of the bad specification brings very specific penalties when incorporated in recruitment advertisements. We will be covering this later.

RESOURCING

The Crucial Choice

Getting your choice, or mix, of recruitment sources right can transform the quality of your recruitment, even if you change nothing else. It can reduce or eliminate recruitment costs, speed the process, produce better candidates, more of them, more easily, with greater certainty.

Some of this will follow from choosing and using sources properly, some from plagiarizing the techniques of the recruitment intermediaries listed below. The sources which come readily to mind include:

- direct advertising
- advertising through an advertising agency
- employment agencies and registers
- direct mail
- recruitment consultants (with or without advertising support)
- search consultants (headhunters)
- volunteers attracted by PR
- outplacement consultants
- contact with local employers shedding people.

Non-recruitment options should also remain in your mind throughout any recruitment exercise, such as:

- taking a calculated risk on promoting someone
- preventing someone leaving
- re-hiring people who have left
- creating a management development climate in which people are happy to accept sideways or even downwards moves in the knowledge that the organization will look after them and they won't lose face.

Correct planning is going to transform your recruitment. Even if you are doing everything 90 per cent right, the extra 10 per cent can be important. If you are doing everything 100 per cent right, there is likely to be someone else involved in the process who is not at the 100 per cent level and may be dragging down your average. This is more true in the later stages, but do not ignore the possibility that one or more of your colleagues are generating errors or omissions which damage your sourcing decisions – perhaps making illicit and imperfect contacts with favourite employment agencies – or just using your approved sources badly!

Plagiarize

In reviewing the activities of the various intermediaries who form a large slice of your potential sources, it is noticeable that they do some things better than, or at any rate, differently from the average in-house recruiter. Not all their work is relevant but there are several points which deserve to be noted and where possible copied or improved on by the employer.

Accepting norms dictated by other employers, the very people you are competing against for staff and labour, is not logical. This falls in the same category as assuming that the salaries at which other people are advertising jobs like yours are correct or that, if correct, they are attracting replies.

There is another compelling reason for trying to do everything right. Only if you have done things well can you use your own sample as a valid indicator of market conditions. Equally, only when your communication with potential candidates has become excellent have you an acceptable base from which to judge their communication failures – if then.

At this point you are going to need a warning from the author, who is commenting on his direct and indirect competitors. No matter how impartial one tries to be in such circumstances, there must be an element of bias and you need to be aware of it. In brief, the author is in favour of advertising through competent, specialist advertising agencies rather than dealing direct with the media (he has tried dealing direct).

He is in favour of using employment agencies, registers, selection consultants and headhunters, but has reservations about search consultants who only offer 'headhunt' when alternative sources or a mix might be more appropriate. For the reasons why, look back to the earlier text and read on.

He also feels that most recruitment can be done *without* the aid of employment agencies, registers, recruitment consultants and headhunters. There is a natural balance: the phrase 'horses for courses' comes to mind.

The Free Sources

There's no free lunch. Similarly the following free sources may involve you in rather more effort than other external help but they won't add much to your direct costs on a recruitment exercise.

Volunteers: come to you because of your corporate reputation, enhanced by past or careful, current PR. Many specialist and local media are desperately short of hard news. If you have anything genuinely newsworthy to say about developments in your organization which implies (or specifically mentions) job opportunities, there is a reasonable chance that you will get a mention (particularly if you have chatted briefly to them on the phone and made it clear that the release is exclusive to them in preference to their direct competitors).

Local redundancy programmes: should be evident from the local press or your own 'bush telegraph'. Pounce the moment redundancies are announced and offer to help, even to the extent of visiting the company and meeting victims on site as a preliminary to inviting them to your place. Everyone benefits.

Outplacement consultants: are also a rich source of instant candidates: many of them handle blue-collar as well as white-collar people. There are now several hundred firms offering outplacement assistance and by the time you read this there will be a UK directory in print, published by the Executive Grapevine team at 79 Manor Way, London SE3 9XG.

Do not equate the use of outplacement assistance with mediocrity. When whole divisions or slices of management are chopped *en masse* there is likely to be a valid sample of good as well as not-so-good employees. Similarly, I have known very high-powered managers pay for the service for themselves to economize on effort and to get professional advice. Furthermore, solo candidates being paid for by the employer can also indicate recognition of past contribution and goodwill rather than a desire to shed the mediocre!

If your product advertising was as bad as your recruitment advertising, wouldn't you fire the sales director?

Advertising – Hits and Myths

Nowadays advertising is both a science and an art form. It is lovingly and professionally created and its results measured. Observance of its basic rules offers reasonable certainty of reliable response levels from consumers.

Unfortunately, this is not true of recruitment advertising. I have never understood why companies whose product advertising reaches the highest possible standards make such basic errors in their recruitment advertising nor why, when the results are unsatisfactory or disastrous, they blame the media, the time of year or a previously unknown skills shortage. None of these are credible culprits. Most recruitment advertising is less than perfect because it is entrusted to amateurs who suffer from one or more of the following:

(a) they do not know the rules
(b) they know the rules but believe that the rules are made to be broken in their special circumstances
(c) they have not thought about the wider context.

To be fair, the rules are not as widely publicized as they ought to be. I can only recall two authoritative studies which the recruiter can quote when trying to fight off those who would interfere with good practice and thus ruin the advertisement. (These philistines, by the way, are referred to in my sector as clients and by personnel people as colleagues, with or without a descriptive adjective!). I shall not bore you with the detail of the studies since most recruiters will be familiar with them. The first was the massive Esso exercise in the late 1960s. The second was the 1988 study commissioned by Price Waterhouse.

Their conclusions, obtained from different directions, were very similar. In some ways, they contradict my contention that advertising is an art form. With recruitment advertising, it does not need to be. The rules are about clear disclosure, not about fancy wording and visual effects. In fact, too much arty input actually detracts from the results.

So far, so good. Put your advertisement, with realistic content, in the appropriate media at an appropriate time and all should follow from there. Alas, it often doesn't. The poor old job seekers, leafing through advertisements, are entitled to wonder if the advertisers are in touch with the real world. Even though the rules have been followed and a salary indicator disclosed, it is sometimes so unrealistic as to be laughable.

Alternatively, the ad is in a wholly unsuitable medium. This is the point at which 'the context' becomes relevant. The general context really applies to all key staff – there is always a shortage of really good people. It follows that if your attempts to find them are penny-pinching, the results will be unsatisfactory. Underkill is the chief reason why otherwise sound ads fail. It is no use putting even the most brilliant ad in the *Mercia Express and Ferret Breeder* if the local readers don't take it seriously as an employment advertising medium. Local media and specialist journals are excellent for certain types of jobs and as supplementary media in support of an insertion in the appropriate national medium, but you can dream up a non-existent skills shortage by relying on them for the wrong jobs.

There is a bonus here for the candidates. They should not ignore their favourite local papers or specialist journals. A response to a lonely ad in one of them could be disproportionately well-received. But the main thrust of the job hunt needs to be in the nationals.

This brings us to another key point. Timing. There is an assumption among advertisers that some times of the year or days of the week are less satisfactory than others. Not so, or not in the way they think. Provided you are looking for people who exist in reasonable numbers, there is a good case for advertising in unpopular weeks or on unpopular days of the week. It is certainly true that the readership (for such ads) is less than at peak times but the number of advertisements usually reduces too, so the competition is less and response rates hold up or may even improve. (This is not so if the national pool of possible respondents is measured only in hundreds – or the preferred medium has a particular day of the week dedicated to ferret breeders.)

Returning to the candidates' interests, there is no particular bonus in the point about timing but there may well be a hidden advantage in the bad ads. From the recruiters' point of view, the bad ad, with inadequate disclosure, generates poor results in two ways: the number of relevant respondents drops sharply sometimes to nil, and the number of irrelevant responses increases. For the serious job hunter who can read between the lines there is a case for replying even to ads which are so uninformative that you cannot be sure that you are relevant to the job. If you do reply and have guessed correctly you may turn yourself into a shortlist of one. There is another reason why recruitment advertisements fail, through no fault of the media used. I discussed earlier the 'infernal triangle' – salary, job content (and context) and candidate specification – but it is sufficiently important to repeat again (and again). *Each must fit with both of the others.* The most common error is not a mismatch on salary, against job or candidate, but a mismatch between job and candidate requirement.

The commonest reason for this is over-specifying the candidate requirement. Far too many managers take the easy option and specify 'A' Levels when they need 'O' Levels, CSEs or nothing. Graduates may be sought when 'A' Levels would be the better indicator. Similarly, 'qualified accountant' is an easy choice for someone who hasn't properly analysed the job and therefore doesn't know that someone in the early stages of the CIMA or ACCA examinations (ie part-qualified, potential ACCAs and ACMAs) would be technically competent.

Perhaps the greatest benefit of the demographic time-bomb is that the resultant shortages will force employers to be more professional about the way they develop candidate specifications. The tendency to specify the ideal candidate rather than the acceptable minimum has always been a problem but the results will get worse, both in wasted advertising expenditure and unhappy job-holders, if recruiters do not recognize the changing market. For those who do, the potential benefits are considerable. People better matched to their jobs should perform better, be happier and may even cost the employer less. As the alternative – sticking stubbornly to demanding, but wrong candidate specifications – will mean being under-staffed or paying a premium to get the wrong people, light may dawn eventually.

A final thought. You may wonder why professional recruiters publish ads which are less than perfect. As indicated above, the clients interfere. One example may suffice. We put out a text recently which gave the client's name but omitted their location.

The chairman was adamant. 'Everyone knows us. Everyone we'd want to hire should know where our head office is.' And he would not be swayed. The first telephone call on the day the ad appeared was brief and to the point. 'I know where the head office is, but where do they hide this job?' We still don't know how many people didn't bother to ask us the question – and didn't reply, either!

Advertising Agencies

Properly used, they offer the nearest thing to a free service you are going to encounter in the recruitment market. They get their revenue in the form of discount from the media and, unless you are big enough to have your own captive agency or use corporate muscle with the media, your best bet is to use a good recruitment advertising agency and even pull back some of the discount in return for disciplined payment and reasonable volumes.

Do get agreement on production costs in advance – a formal rate card would be appropriate – and make it clear to them that your continued loyalty depends on being given good advice about specialist and local media where they are more cost effective than the nationals. The same applies to cheap nationals versus expensive ones: and to sensible, modest, space decisions. If this rule is not made clear you will end up with massive expenditures on big ads in expensive Sunday papers when smaller spaces in cheaper media would be equally effective, or even more effective.

In spite of this caveat, the good agency is capable of transforming your advertising. For instance, advertisements properly set (trade set, rather than paper set) can improve impact and make your organization look more professional. Agency advice on key ingredients and copy can make sure your advertisements are better than the uninformative or boring ones you are competing against. Brief them, in writing, that they are to act as a final filter on matters of employment law and good practice and you may avoid unpleasant equal opportunity lapses caused by one of your colleagues' amateur attempts at writing or 'improving' copy.

Equally, they know that their competitors know who is handling your advertising so they will usually be pleased to help you restrain your colleagues' verbosity and imprecision on copy and style. Even a chairman who won't listen to *you* may take advice from outside.

Finally, if they are communicating well with their other clients, they may give you accurate forecasts of the likely response and have inventive alternatives to suggest in difficult situations. The author's favourite agency, on volume recruitment for other clients, has successfully recommended direct mail, radio, TV and posters.

Even a chairman who won't listen to *you*
may take advice from outside

Employment Agencies

The author has a liking for service businesses where the objectives of the business and the customer, although not necessarily identical, are not in conflict and at least point in the same direction. Employment agencies have a problem in this regard. Most of them run on a no-sale, no-pay fee structure which mitigates against quality performance. It may have a superficial and transient effect on motivation but this is quickly eroded. How would you like a business where the customers and the product are both unfaithful to you?

Intelligent employer-recruiters can turn this to corporate advantage. Their corporate objectives are probably to hire good-quality people quickly and reliably, with no money wasted on abortive ads or, much worse, wrong employees. The agency objectives include:

- selling as many of the candidates they meet as possible
- attracting more
- filling all the vacancies registered
- filling (perhaps even by creating them) vacancies not registered
- *and* getting paid for all this.

Unfortunately, other things being equal, *most* of the effort employment agencies expend on candidates and vacancies does not get paid for, because:

(a) candidates find jobs through other agencies or direct advertisements
(b) candidates decide not to change jobs after all
(c) some candidates prove virtually unemployable
(d) customers fill jobs from other sources
(e) customers decide not to fill some jobs
(f) some jobs cannot be filled by the sort of candidate sought, because the candidate specification is wrong
(g) some customers try to avoid paying the agency fees
(h) some candidates leave or get fired during the warranty period.

Selection Consultants

The main problem when choosing a selection consultant is to find out what each firm actually does. They range from the equivalent of employment agencies to search consultants, with a diverse mix of competence and techniques.

Some neither select nor consult and one of the multi-branch 'consultancies' has been known to handle an assignment without meeting the clients or the candidates. At the other end of the scale, some of the smaller independents employ a menu of sourcing options wider than any client company might envisage, which could include any or all of the following:

- file search on computerized database
- advertising
- partial headhunt
- liaison with outplacement consultants
- soliciting editorial mentions in national media
- assessing internal candidates (if appropriate).

Charges vary too. The majority do not work on an agency basis (no sale, no pay) but the pattern of stage payments varies dramatically and not always in line with the quality, quantity or service offered.

It is impossible to give absolute guidelines but if you want to delegate to a selection consultancy with any certainty of getting good results there are several basic indicators to watch out for.

- 'success-only' fees probably indicate an agency rather than consultancy approach, whatever the brochures claim, similarly
- an unwillingness to meet the client
- forecasting 'shortlists' in days rather than weeks implies a paper-pushing exercise rather than a selection process
- if you ask how many candidates per vacancy and you receive numbers higher than, say, six, the probable implication is that the firm is going to throw at you every candidate who comes close to the minimum specification: if this is what you want, fine, but do not assume that any or all of them will match your ideal.

43

None of this is an argument against any level of service, just a reminder that you should find out in advance what you are going to get and decide whether it is appropriate to your current need. There is no point in paying agency fees, or their advertising costs, if the problem could be solved by cost-effective advertising with the aid of a competent recruitment advertising agency.

Some 'consultancies' share the lesser ad agencies' weakness for very large ads because they improve the consultancies' image, and you will pay more to advertise through them than you would to go it alone. Similarly, their media choice may reflect a desire to gather bodies who can be sold later to other clients, rather than a proper concern for your immediate need. Their ad agencies are happy about this because they sell more space, so there is nobody on your side.

Recently the author observed a classic example of this when a distinguished client insisted that the advertising, which every-one agreed was a necessary part of the recruitment process, was placed in the agreed medium (no dispute about the correct medium, either) through the client's advertising agency, as an economy measure. This seemed logical until we found that the 'service' involved:

- failing to supply proofs to the clients
- failing to check proofs, so that several spelling errors and an incorrect reference went to press
- using at least 30 per cent more space than was needed
- having the ad badly set (probably by the paper) to save money, but at the expense of impact and possible response.

This is, of course, a complaint against advertising agencies rather than consultancies, but the lesson remains – be sure of what you are buying; the final quality control is in your hands.

The same applies to the warranty. Ask what happens if candidates leave or prove unsuitable after joining. There is considerable variation amongst the firms, from the basic agency type terms which merely refund a fraction of your fee for depar-tures in the first six to eight weeks, through to the three or six months free replacement warranty of the more thorough consul-tancies. If you don't like the warranty, negotiate at the *beginning* of the assignment when your leverage is greatest, not just before you make the appointment.

Executive Search

Headhunters come in all shapes and sizes. Although in a people-based business, they themselves are not particularly gregarious and signally fail to achieve common views with their competitors about the practice of executive search. If there were a collective noun for them it would probably be a 'disagreement of headhunters'! It is very important that you know the areas of disagreement because they have a substantial effect on the services you buy.

There are several key questions to ask:

Charging: in addition to the gross fee it is important to find out what extras may be included, particularly if long distance travel by candidates or consultants is involved. Assuming that second-class rail travel is the norm may lead to a nasty shock if everyone flies first-class from Scotland to England. Also ask how the fee stages are earned. The retainer point is easy but some consultants charge the second tranche only when a shortlist has been generated, others at the thirty-day mark. The third stage is even more variable. With some, this is only charged when a candidate accepts the offer of employment. With others the issue of an offer is enough. Yet others do it automatically in the third month of the assignment. There are also significant differences about the amount of work they are prepared to do after the first short list and/or offer fails. Ask, and get the answer in writing if it sounds at all equivocal. Also ask what guarantees they give if the candidate leaves or has to be fired in the first year . . .

Shortlists: may be anything from one to six or more people. Ask – not just for fee purposes – what they regard as the norm and the minimum. Ask also what best and worst timing they forecast and, indeed, what sort of data you may get at shortlist stage.

Ethics: are important for two reasons. First, you need to know to what extent your organization is protected in the near future as a result of using a firm of headhunters. How wide is the bar on

Find out what extras may be included . . .

poaching? And for how long? Second and conversely, do their ethics prevent them from searching in companies which would be natural nurseries for the sort of person you seek? This leads us naturally to the subject of –

Researchers: who are a very important part of the service. They can be internal employees, external sub-contract workers (dedicated to the firm or freelance) or the consultants themselves. Note whether they come to briefing meetings (all second-hand communication is imperfect) and ask whether they are subject to any other ethical constraints which make them less than ideal. For example, some regard it as ethically unacceptable to re-use the results of research for a different client within a specified time-scale. This turns relevant knowledge into a block rather than a bonus.

Specialization: is, therefore, a mixed blessing. You need to ask questions which indicate whether the consultants know what you're talking about and then make sure that they, and their researchers, are not inhibited by their recent work.

Methods: are more diverse than you might expect. There should always be a mixture of file search and desk research, but specialization may induce an undue dependence on files at the expense of true research. There are few searches where you can be sure that all the possible candidates have been identified. For example, if you think that on a pan-European search run by a firm with branches in every capital city they have managed to motivate the relevant team members in each country to join in on your behalf, you are an optimist. Ask how they benefit from the European network and keep on asking until you get solid, factual answers.

Ask also whether an advertisement would complement the search and listen carefully to the reply. Those who are wholly dedicated to search may have closed minds on this. It is important that you know whether the clients' interests or their house policies take precedence. Ask – just for laughs – what other ethical or practical constraints may inhibit their work on your behalf. I don't know what answer you'll get, but if you don't ask sure as hell it won't be volunteered!

47

The hidden penalties

There are two more things you need to know about headhunting and these can cost a lot of time and money, which is a pity because headhunting can be cheaper than selection consultancy fees plus national advertising costs, at all but very senior levels. The two hidden traps balance out this advantage.

One is that, because the employer is the 'applicant', the candidates quite rightly expect to be able to negotiate a premium for their services, by contrast with the advertised vacancy where *they* have declared themselves to be in the job hunting market.

Worse, they are able to maintain this posture throughout the selection process. It is vitally important that all those in the employing organization who are involved in the selection process are very clearly briefed about the implications of this.

New users of headhunting are particularly prone to misunderstand this and remain fixed in their old grooves expecting the candidate to show why the organization should consider them, while the candidate, quite rightly, demands that the organization follows through its approach with a compelling reason why the candidate should be interested.

Unless this is sorted out very early on, the employers' representatives will reject the candidate as under-motivated and the candidate will decide that the interviewers are conceited buffoons, out of touch with reality. This usually ruins the exercise because neither side will then move from the original position.

The author's competitors allege that professional practices are particularly bad on this point!

Good communication implies brevity;
all verbiage beyond the core message
reduces the chance of comprehension

'Well, are we broke or aren't we?'

Better Communication Through Better Documentation

Candidates (unless desperate) will not accept an offer of employment unless you have made a reasonable case for the job and for your organization. This demands excellence in documentation at all stages:

- the internal job description and candidate specification
- the wider, and perhaps simpler document you issue to candidates *before* interview which also describes the company and structure
- all the letters you write to candidates
- the advertisement
- the application form
- the offer and any appendices.

Recruitment is a marketing exercise, not an obstacle course. Unless *your* communication is excellent you cannot judge applicants by *their* communication weaknesses – with the possible exception of candidates for a job to improve communications in some way! (If your errors or omissions are gross, even they may decide that the underlying problem is insuperable.) There is a bonus. The more discriminating the candidates, the more likely it is that they will respond to excellence in this area and warm to you rather than pursuing those companies who are competing against you for their services.

Best practice is likely to yield best results, and serves both your qualitative needs and the financial objective of getting the right number of people, in the right place, at the right time, at the right price. You can even carry the production purchasing analogy a trifle further and plan for a 'just-in-time' programme. This is actually making a virtue out of necessity, for some recruitment will always have to be carried out at short notice when key people leave and, in spite of all your people development plans, there is no possible internal successor.

Poor communication is the major enemy in all this. Just so you can fully appreciate the potential for improvement, let us consider the potential downside of any form of communication which is less than satisfactory:

- no reply, from good candidates
- the wrong reply, from good and bad
- loss of the best candidates at any stage
- retention of interest of the worst
- your staff's time wasted with no-hopers (and they, too, value their time)
- marginal people are interviewed because good ones are scarce
- perceived discrimination leads to a tribunal case
- future recruitment is damaged by current errors which are remembered by candidates and casual readers
- gross errors may lose you customers or community goodwill
- specialized errors may generate a complaint to the Data Protection Registrar
- agencies and consultancies helping you may be misdirected or demotivated.

All this is avoidable. As we consider the three key groups of documents – specification, advertisement and letters – the potential benefits should become clearer and their practical and monetary value evident.

Job description and candidate specification

As indicated earlier, this document is important in ensuring that all parties involved within the organization agree about the real requirement (make them initial it). However, it is often written in corporate language which needs to be simplified and abbreviated for outsiders. In addition, some description of the organization has to be included to make it an effective marketing document for candidates. Although it may be a pain in the neck when you are busy, producing this document properly is an economy of effort reducing time spent briefing each candidate and enabling you to assess later how each has reacted to identical input.

Advertisement

Even if your favourite advertising agency or an enthusiastic colleague is writing the advertising copy, someone has to vet the result. The person who writes the copy is too close and cannot always see how the words will be interpreted by an outsider. In any case, you may be paying up to £20 per word for it. Get value for money. Avoid verbosity, duplication and jargon. Maximize disclosure. Don't hide key data – even unpleasant matters – every problem is a USP to somebody, whether it be location, travel, chaotic or prosaic job content. Make sure your preferred candidates realize the ad is aimed at them. Encourage replies. Encourage disclosure by candidates in their initial response. Always remember the ad will appear among dozens, if not hundreds, of others. Yours must compel attention. People will not reply to it unless they are motivated to read it, by clear and attractive headings, good layout and typefaces and bold borders.

Letters

This is not the place to attempt a comprehensive guide to business correspondence, but you may find it helpful to study past recruitment letters emanating from your colleagues or your own department and consider whether they meet the following criteria:

- are they good PR for the organization?
- would they encourage applicants to apply again?
- have they mentioned, if relevant, other opportunities elsewhere in the organization?
- would they encourage current or potential customers and suppliers to deal with you?
- If the applicants look good but are not relevant this time, have they been told what would make them appropriate next year?
- does every letter clearly tell the applicants what you are doing next and what they have to do?
- do your letters to your advisors (agencies and consultants) achieve the same standards?

Word processors give you a magnificent opportunity to be mechanically personal and caring, without effort. It would be a shame to waste one of the few free gifts which technology has to offer.

Do be sure that letters are appropriate. Letters, in some circumstances, are for people who lack interpersonal skills or whose poor time management prevents them using the telephone. The telephone provides instant response and some potential for starting, or continuing, the selection process. It also makes candidates feel you are efficient and you care.

PROCESSING

Processing

This section starts at the point when you have lit the fuse on the sourcing procedure, whether by advertising or delegating to some external agency (or your network of employees, friends and families), and await your first contact with candidates. There is a lull, which can be used most effectively to do some for-ward planning. For example, you could consider the following:

- formulating a contingency plan for swift remedial action if the response quality or quantity is not adequate
- clearing your diary, and the diaries of all others involved, for the period when you plan to interview. Initially, many of your colleagues may resent this discipline because they don't believe that there will be a supply of candidates at that future date. This is something you can only cure by example; in other words, keep on doing it right and they will learn – the under-lying principle is sound
- planning for the decision date and for the offer date – not least so that those involved are on site! Create a climate of good timing.

All this may seem terribly basic but there is a widespread reluctance among otherwise sensible managers to make time for recruitment matters because they are too busy. Since they are too busy because they are short-staffed, this is a self-perpetuat-ing situation. Break the chain. Improving recruitment priorities enables earlier relief.

There is another good reason for doing everything promptly. Delay is a major enemy of good recruitment. A lost day here or there loses weeks or months if you miss media deadlines. Delayed interviews demotivate candidates and delayed offers lose people to more decisive employers or put their start dates back a month because of notice problems. One of your aims is not to lose anybody by error or delay. Brisk processing is good marketing. It improves your image to the candidates who are, as indicated elsewhere, potential customers, suppliers and ambassadors for your organization. How much easier to process the people you've got in the first wave than to start remedial action because they've withered away.

However, if you *do* need to take remedial action, be sure you know that instant action will bring extra candidates on stream at the same time as the existing sample. For instance, if you started with a low-budget direct advertising campaign, it may be sensible to add candidates from slightly more expensive sources (agencies, or small 'national' ads) rather than have to do the exercise twice. This is usually better than weakening on the quality front and meeting people whose records look marginal. People are seldom better than their track records, and there are usually better things you can do with your time than interviewing people who patently do not meet the specification.

In pursuit of this philosophy, the ideal is that the advertisement reply instructions (or the recruitment consultants' output) will have been so good that you can make interview decisions without going through the process of getting an application form completed. If this is not possible, it is essential that something is done to retain the interest of all the worthwhile candidates until the interview, or your decision not to interview them.

As indicated earlier, this could include sending out a good brief on the job and organization. It also includes making early and flexible interview arrangements, which get double-checked (make on the phone and confirm in writing) and are not easily confused. Specify the day of the week, date, time, place, whom they are to see and how long the meeting may take. Send a map. Mention public transport facilities and/or parking arrangements. If you are going to pay travel expenses subject to reasonable limits, specify what those limits are. For instance, if someone makes the decision that it is easier to fly both ways to save the cost of an overnight stay, clear it in advance. Squabbling later when the house rules have been exceeded may damage your relationship with an otherwise sound candidate.

Finally, remind your own people about the meetings and make doubly sure that the times are being protected!

Bad Form

The application form is one of the most counter-productive tools in the recruitment process. If used *traditionally,* it alienates candidates without enhancing the quality of selection. Unless the application form can be improved and used better it may be better to do without them and gain the goodwill of all the candidates who dislike having to complete them. However, this is an undisciplined compromise.

The exciting thing about the present norms in the design and use of application forms is that standards are so low that you must be able to improve some aspect of your present practice – and the results it generates.

Many of the ills of the form stem from the fact that, later in the process, it is an important document for the record. Alas, this tends to obscure and obstruct its earlier purpose as a communication aid in the selection process. If we focus on this, there are several things it has to do better, such as:

- encouraging people to complete and return it
- being simple to complete
- permitting people to use a good CV as a partial substitute
- generating data relevant to the current vacancy
- compelling exception reporting on points not covered in CVs.

To achieve this we need to drag the average form up from the primeval norm to an acceptable minimum standard. You can probably do this better than the author, but the following guidelines may be a useful start to the list:

- does it comply with current equal opportunity rules?
- and IPM advice?
- does the layout permit people to type their text?
- can people with full CVs understand which bits of the form they can ignore? (Clear and early instructions on this point may improve the chance that they will complete the rest properly)

- is it legible without a magnifying glass?
- is it free of ambiguous words and jargon?
- is the reply address on the form, as well as your covering letter?
- is it in all other respects user-friendly?

That list should produce a better norm. To climb *above* the norm how about:

- does the form ask for signs of excellence?
- does it include questions which make candidates think? (For instance, how the applicant differs from, or is better than peers; any interests, aptitudes, skills not evident from track record or omitted from CV on grounds of modesty or space)
- is some part of the form, or an appendix, specifically devoted to applicants' relevance to the vacancy?

This last point is the major omission on most application forms today. Providing candidates with a clear indication of the minimum candidate specification and inviting an itemized response, using questions which solicit factual and qualitative replies must help both candidates and recruiters.

There are several other things you can do to encourage response, especially on jobs where you have spent a mint in the knowledge that the response will be slim – at best. Try

- a Freepost reply address or
- a large, addressed reply envelope (stamped)
- send them a job brief which retains their interest, tempts reply and helps them to realize they are very relevant (if they are), or wasting their time (if they are not). Self selection saves your time and probably enhances their view of your corporate professionalism for the future.

Good practice in this area can vaccinate candidates against the common (adverse) reaction to application forms, particularly if you can minimize the cases where use of, or full completion of, the form is demanded. In consequence the yield per vacancy should rise appreciably.

Your application form – is it legible without
a magnifying glass?

Interviewing

Opinions about the value of interviews are sharply divided. Most people consider them an essential part of the selection process. A growing minority considers they have absolutely no validity as an objective guide to future work performance.

Both views are understandable: they may not be mutually exclusive. But, if the interview is not satisfactory as a primary filter in recruitment, we need to be aware what it is, or can be made to be, and we need to complement it with earlier or parallel filters.

The Deceivers

Before we do this – particularly if you or your colleagues currently feel comfortable with the interview process – it is important that you recognize how many people have a vested interest in hiding something about themselves. Study the list below and think how few, if any, you could spot in the course of a conventional interview:

Actors
Bigamists
Con-men
Drunks
Erotomaniacs
Fraudsters
Gold-diggers
Heroin addicts
Infanticides
Jokers (practical)
Kleptomaniacs
Liars
Misogynists
Nihilists
Opportunists
Pyromaniacs

Quarrelsome types
Recidivists
Spies
Technophobes
Untidy slobs
Valetudinarians
Wimps
Xenophobes

This entirely omits the many thousands who have put a cosmetic gloss on their track records, omitted brief past jobs, exaggerated past authority and generally hope your reference checking won't be too thorough!

Other Variables

Even if we acquit the average candidate of any intent to suppress or distort information, we must recognize that there are too many variables in the interview process. For instance:

- some candidates are better interview performers than others, and vice versa
- some candidates have more physical presence than others
- nearly all candidates are affected by the pressures of recent (or future) events
- your conduct of the interview is likely to vary, no matter how hard you try to be consistent
- your perception of someone in a sequence of candidates is likely to shift according to the merits of the preceding and the subsequent examples!

Possible Improvements

What can we do to improve the process? Complementary filters like better reference-checking, tests, better selection before interview, better exchange of information, medical examinations, and scored bio-data are dealt with elsewhere, so we can concentrate on the conduct of the interview and its objectives. If we accept how unsatisfactory it is as a predictor of performance, there are still many things to work on, including:

- a chance for future colleagues to test 'personal chemistry'
- better briefing for the candidate
- structured data collection to complement prior paperwork
- work samples

. . . a cosmetic gloss on their track records

All of these are possible, even at managerial level. And if you improve the quality of the process, you can afford to run fewer interviews, better. This affords a bonus for recruiter and candidate. If you are able to be ruthless about the interview programme, because the sourcing and the issue of information to the candidates ensures that you only interview people who meet the specification and are actively interested in the job, you have the luxury of reviewing the few front-runners in greater depth, rather than seeing dozens in desperation.

Broad Principles

We can attempt improvement on two levels. First, the macro or conceptual. I cannot stress too strongly how your questions should reflect the 'work sample' aspect. Every time you stray to the 'soft', peripheral question you waste time and degrade the quality of the discussion. Save the hobbies, family and school questions to the end, or next time, or never. Develop and use questions which attack the core of the job need and directly (or more probably indirectly) permit *you* to answer questions like:

- how intelligent are they?
- can they remember the second part of a two-part question?
- what would they do in the job if so and so happened?
- what impact did they make on past problems?
- which bits of the job interest them? And why?
- what aspects of the job would they have to brush up on?
- can they use a PC? Can you let them show their fluency?
- do they listen well?
- do they express themselves well?
- do they understand difficult words which, in your environment, are commonplace?
- do their criteria for past companies' and colleagues' performance reflect *your* company's?
- how do they think through a problem?
- what gives them job satisfaction?
- how do they motivate others?

And so on . . .

Fine Tuning

Secondly, on the micro, practical level, here is some good advice plagiarized from a firm of outplacement consultants, on the basis of their candidates' experiences!

Can they use a PC?

- be yourself and treat candidates as fellow humans
- relax candidates. They'll reveal more. This demands a sympathetic environment and privacy, with nil interruption
- read their records first: plan your probes
- don't interview across a desk
- listen. Don't make statements – ask questions. Listen again
- standardize your *stock* questions so all candidates are responding to the same form of words
- control the meeting
- be explicit about your objectives for the meeting and the data you want, but
- use open-ended questions, not yes/no examples
- ask questions which tempt a qualitative response – values and attitudes
- don't volunteer judgements, ie don't agree or disagree with their contribution for comfort's sake
- but use sympathetic noises to encourage further disclosure . . . or a nod instead of a grunt!
- take them back if they deviate on key answers
- don't give them answers. This is not about multiple-choice questions!
- do show interest. Even read up enough about body language to give interested signals. Smile
- use short questions. Keep *them* talking
- don't be afraid to show ignorance and ask for elucidation
- ask for evidence of excellence
- look for what candidates have, which your team lacks
- look for what they *have,* not just what's missing
- note enthusiasm
- note and record any objective evidence of
    - intellectual application
    - emotional maturity/stability
    - human relations skills (and empathy)
    - insight into self and others
- consider the quality and range of their questions
- don't use panel interviews!

Finally, avoid gratuitous error. Think of all the things which have been done to you and colleagues and make sure you, and they, are avoiding them!

I have one other piece of advice. It is a technique I use which surprised my colleagues at a recent training session, but I've

Relax the candidates . . . smile . . .

been using it for years, and now they have embraced it. If you are ruthless about only meeting properly pre-selected people, you can usually identify during an interview if the candidate does not meet the specification, or is substantially weaker in one or two areas than people you've already seen. Tell them – explicitly – that in this context they are 80/90 per cent right but you have formed the view that they are light on X and perhaps Y. This has three great merits. If you are wrong, they have a chance to correct it. If you are right, they know why and don't have to worry about unknown problems ranging from dress to BO. Lastly, you don't have to keep them on the hook and write later!

Almost invariably, candidates are grateful and it clears the air for future contact. This is important because every interview is an investment. Even if you don't hire people now, the interview may help you decide whether they will respond to a future approach when the right job comes up – or the existing vacancy changes so it *does* fit them!

Alas, you are probably blessed with colleagues who are not likely to read the foregoing text, and are wholly unwilling to read the IPM book *Interviews: skills and strategy*, which contains a heavier slice of the author's recommendations on the subject. For them, it may be that a checklist is the correct answer – so here is a summary, with which you can amplify those parts of the preceding text which you regard as workable in your own environment! What follows may repeat other bits of the book but it is included on the 'what I say three times is true' principle!

The Good Interview Checklist
The objective
Are all involved parties (including the candidate) clear about the primary objective, which is to determine how the candidate will perform for the company in this job, or another – now or in the future?

It is not about finding reasons to reject.

Secondary objectives
Are all parties on your side aware that the candidates may be customers, suppliers, ambassadors for your organization or, if badly treated, deadly enemies for life?

Do they recognize that the possibility of using the candidates in the future imposes a massive need to make objective and adequate notes; and that these should contain facts, not just opinions, because the facts will probably remain unchanged whereas the opinions may not be relevant in a later context?

Prior action
In spite of the administrative burden, has someone taken action beforehand to maximize the value of the interview process:

- by confirming the timing, context, duration and location of the interview? This includes specifying day of week and date, whom they are to meet, transport facilities, map, parking, etc, and double-checking by phone – if the arrangements are by letter – or confirming in writing, if arranged by phone. Do not, for instance, just say 'next' Friday. To many people next Friday is less than a week away – to others, more.
- by trying to exchange data in both directions? Offer a good brief on organization, job and candidate requirement. Good disclosure by the organization can enhance the candidate's input, or avoid a totally wasted meeting. Ask for ways they fit the spec. Ask for evidence of their qualifications.

Environment
Can this be quiet, non-threatening, uninterrupted and comfy?

Participants
Will this be just interviewer and victim, or several interviewers? Have you considered how the process could be improved by doing some of the briefing beforehand by audio-visuals, or video? If several people want or need to review the candidate – without the horrors of a panel interview – could this be achieved with joint interviewers, one of whom listens rather than inter-rupts? (This is actually a very effective technique. It also reduces the risk that you run the same interview several times so that the candidate's performance, or opinion of you, goes sour.)

Questions
Have you all developed, in advance, questions to ask the candidate which enable you to:

- answer all the questions you must later ask yourself?
- fill all the gaps in the candidate's data offering?

Do your colleagues understand the pitfalls posed by discrimina-tory questions? (Do they have any understanding of current employment law?)

Is everyone involved aware that offering their opinions to the candidate wastes time in which they could be listening, or asking questions?

If their questions do not assist you to assess the candidate's comprehension, memory, logic, management attitudes, intelligence, experience, skills or interests, why are they being asked at all?

Are we at all times remembering that the candidates can help us in the selection process? Listen to *their* questions. Be prepared to adapt your supplementary questions to explore areas of concern (yours and theirs).

Learn from accountants (yes, there is life beyond the security screen) – practise exception reporting. Make it clear to the candidates that the rule applies on both sides. If they do not conform, you are entitled to consider whether you would suffer brain damage working with them. You then dismiss this unchristian thought and tell them again – more clearly!

Admin.

There are several obligatory points:

- do make sure you verify who the candidate is (clearly enunciate the name on your paperwork)
- make *your* identity clear
- note and retain all promises and predictions made during *all* the meetings: the candidates will recall them clearly!
- at the start, tell them what is to happen: recap later
- ask if they are interested in the job, do not assume it
- on the exception reporting trail, ask them to identify the things which modesty, space, or lack of knowledge of the job and environment, led them to omit from their CVs
- *ask* if they have other offers in process, and the timing
- *ask* when they could join
- check their availability for the next meeting and tell them why
- check their current rewards package and range of expectations in future jobs
- tell them what happens next
- at managerial level, ask them to do, send or deliver something . . . this is a work sample
- ask them to let you know if their situation changes
- thank them for coming
- engage them in conversation as they leave: this is the time afterthoughts come to the surface – theirs and yours.

Afterthoughts

This checklist was exposed to numerous people in the selection business and they suggested several additions which the author is entirely prepared to admit he had forgotten or had not thought of at all!

- disclose problems during your briefing of the candidate: good candidates will be attracted by them, weak ones repulsed
- but do *sell* the company and job; do not assume the candidates know all your corporate good points
- excite them with what they could achieve
- don't filter by a series of interviews so that X sees all ten people and eliminates five, Y meets them and passes two to Z who dislikes both (but would have hired one of the people that X has turned down . . .)
- do not consume alcohol in the half day before an interview. You will think better, listen better and speak more clearly without it.

Interviews are like tennis. They are influenced by your form on the day, by the other player, the weather, time pressures, health, hangovers, your opponent's problems . . . and the state of the grass.

Selection

The first constraint in the selection process is that you may not be able to afford the luxury of selection. There are many cases when organizations desperately need people and recruitment is the only solution. In these circumstances everyone who meets the minimum criteria will come under offer. In some ways this is a more demanding exercise since it is even more important to set the minimum limits correctly and to ensure that the candidates meet them.

The second constraint is the existence of a number of traditional selection aids which you would do well to ignore (and make sure that your colleagues are not surreptitiously depending on them). They include:

- gut feel
- a belief that the candidate is nice
- reliance on unstructured unscientific interviews
- graphology
- astrology
- phrenology
- palmistry
- colour selection preferences
- certain proprietary ipsative tests
- love at first sight (not quite the same as gut feel)
- reading entrails (although a medical examination can be a useful supplement).

Before we explore the approved list, it may be as well to remember why people make silly judgements through subjective methods. In brief, one prerequisite for any selection process is a reasonable sample from which to choose. Get the supply right and mistakes born of desperation (and some arising from prejudices) are easier to eliminate.

Once you have got your supply of candidates, introduce a new rule, either by dictate if you are in charge, or by example and logic if you are 'pig in the middle'. The rule is fairly innocuous: it consists of asking for *facts* rather than just opinions. We live in a virtually fact-free society in which the media have great fun presenting opinions instead of facts. There are even programmes where people offer opinions upon other people's opinions, untarnished by any sign of a fact. Selection demands better than this. Ask, and keep on asking, for the facts upon which your colleagues base their opinions. Ask that they put them in writing, in the knowledge that there will be some form of post-audit. Compare the facts. Note the different opinions flowing from the same set of facts, or from two overlapping halves of the same facts, when neither colleague has elicited the full picture.

This is salutary in several ways. The results should tempt you to improve both your data collection and your deductions there-after. It may convince your colleagues. It may also tempt all those involved to seek better ways of assessing people than by conventional interviews.

You could also make the point that the quality of data gathered depends to some extent on the quality of the questions which generated it. The better the question, the better the chance of a worthwhile answer. (The reverse side of this coin is enshrined in computer parlance – 'rubbish in rubbish out'.)

The same principle applies to requests and instructions, like:

- requests for candidates to do something at, before, or after interview
- reply instructions, application forms, tests
- your brief to consultants
- your letters to candidates
- instructions to colleagues about interview practice.

Don't get the idea that by including instructions to colleagues the book implies that there is some way you can impose an iron discipline upon the conduct of all interviews and all subsequent selection decisions. You will not find such a recipe, for two reasons.

The first is that it isn't that sort of book. This is a DIY book, not a pile of completed 'off-the-peg' recipes for success. It provides a menu – or shopping basket – of thought-starters for you to use and adapt.

The second reason is that it wouldn't work. You are going to have enough trouble getting a few, very basic points agreed and implemented. Total unanimity is a pipe-dream. But a core of common practice may be one of the most important contributions to improvements in the selection process and thus your total choice and use of people.

One breakthrough on this front could be to introduce a sense of proportion about interviews and a desire to improve them. If you can temper your colleagues' dependence on interviews, in your capacity as the one sane person in the madhouse, further benefits will flow. At this point, a ray of light for those who believe in the interview. There are some circumstances when you are permitted – even encouraged – to use the interview:

- to identify personal chemistry between boss and potential employee
- to identify the presence or lack of interpersonal skills in people being selected for 'front of house' jobs
- for data gathering and the resolution of queries arising from candidates' CVs
- to assess basic comprehension
- to assess use of English or use of other languages, where necessary
- to ascertain quality of thought (subject to certain disciplines)
- to elicit the candidates' reasons for being hired
- to identify whether they are interested in the job
- to test memory (can they remember the third part of a three-part question?)
- to assess the quality of their questions
- to judge their reactions to sample problems (this is getting into the work sample area).

All of these are acceptable criteria for the selection decision, but do please consider complementing them with the results of tests, references, and formal work samples. They may help to eliminate the sort of dialogue which follows (only the names have been changed to protect the guilty):

'That last candidate is useless. I don't know why you wanted me to see him. Is there anyone else?'

'George, that was the best candidate. What was wrong?'

'Well he couldn't even answer a few simple questions. Half his answers were rubbish. He's thick.'

'George, you never ask simple questions. What was wrong with the answers?'

'Twice he said something completely irrelevant to the question. I tell you he's not good enough.'

'How was he otherwise?'

'I suppose pretty reasonable, but the moment I heard him spout rubbish I just gave up. And he smokes.'

'George, did you have the window open?'

'Of course. I told you he smokes. I always open the window before I ask people if they smoke. What's that got to do with it?'

'The noise level outside today was pretty high.'

'So?'

'George, we've got one good candidate . . .'

'He isn't good; he's thick or inattentive.'

'We've got one good candidate and we cannot afford to lose him.'

'I interviewed him just the way I always do, just like the rest.'

'No you didn't. I've heard you in action. You ask convoluted, rhetorical questions whenever you're playing for time and you always play for time when the questions coming back at you get tricky. The double negatives creep in, and you retreat to your worst slice of Geordie. What with that and the racket outside, he probably didn't hear the question properly or, if he did, he couldn't puzzle it out.'

'Well, that's as maybe, but I still think he's thick.'

'George, you've done this to us before. You thought he was alright for the first hour or you would have thrown him out in half the time, now, wouldn't you?'

'Perhaps, but you weren't there.'

'No I wasn't, because I was scoring the test he did earlier. He's got an IQ almost as high as yours' (actually it was higher but this didn't seem the right moment to introduce the point) 'and he may be slightly deaf but a medical will soon sort that out. Give him the benefit of the doubt, otherwise we'll have to do the whole exercise again and it'll be an extra month before you can get anyone on board. Now, did you like him until the, er, misunderstanding? If so, will you let Celia have a look at him before he goes?'

'He's gone. But I suppose you may be right. Yes, alright, but it'll take an age to get him back. He's working very hard at the moment.'

74

'Just your sort, really George? And he hasn't gone. We headed him off at reception and he's asking difficult questions in the showroom. I'll take him up to Celia. While I'm doing that, you might give thought to what sort of offer we could make him!'

With friends like George, who needs enemies? George, incidentally, is quite a reasonable person but he doesn't like interviews – or he alleges he doesn't. Nevertheless, he relies on them implicitly if he is conducting them: that is he *did*, until Chris, by a long series of confrontations like the one above, weaned him away from total dependence on *bad* interviews.

The power of the test is that it is authoritative. Unless your colleagues are totally pig-headed, the results of a well validated, formal, normative test carry greater authority than most people's interview results. This is not an argument for discarding the interview. By all means let your team aim for improvements, but given the availability of simple, short, non-threatening tests on:

- IQ
- the application of intelligence
- personality factors
- management style
- interests and
- skills

there is little merit in preferring the subjective interview result to the output of an objective test. It is an uphill struggle to get this point accepted, but it pays. The most compelling argument may be that it cuts down the number of interviews you have to conduct and the time per interview. Alternatively, colleagues can spend just as much time, but to better effect. Incidentally, you may have noted that the test results were not made available *before* the interview. This is not just a matter of logistics. Releasing the results to the interviewer in advance is not, on balance, a good thing. There is some evidence that, rather than helping by pointing at areas to probe, it actually tends to prejudice the direction and results of the meeting. The author also suspects that the interviewer works harder at being objective and of recording results and reasons, if he or she knows the interview output is going to be scrutinized against some objective set of benchmarks.

Post-audit is another possible tool for sharpening up the long-term selection pattern. Given that the discipline of creating and retaining interview assessments and test results has been accepted, it is much easier to go back and see whether people performed the way that was predicted. Knowing that the post-audit is going to happen also forces interviewers to make predictions in an acceptable format.

However, unless this has already been done, you may have to start with fairly slim data. Nevertheless, *do* start – possibly by attempting a review of people currently leaving or proving less than satisfactory. If there isn't enough data, this is a useful argument for making sure that the omission is corrected in respect of current and future hirings.

This too, is going to be an uphill struggle. Managers have no incentive to disclose mediocre hirings unless these are very bad or they can blame someone else for the decision! Create a climate in which they know that nemesis is just around the corner and they might as well be the ones to raise the matter rather than pretending that someone's sub-standard performance comes as a complete surprise to them. The 'no surprises' philosophy has its place in people matters as well as in financial reporting. After all, people produce the results (or lack thereof), and they will also produce the surprises unless they are motivated to disclose, discuss and correct promptly.

While you are at it, you might take a look at the extent to which disclosure is working. One of the author's favourite American clients, new to UK management practice, was asking about differences he had noticed between practice 'Stateside' and in the newly acquired UK subsidiaries. He was happy about the level of disclosure of impending problems, but surprised that the new teams brought him only problems, when he was used to the home team telling him about problems *and* what they had done, or were about to do, to solve them. It was pointed out to him that this said more about the previous managements of those subsidiaries than about UK practice in general. However, you may feel this is a common problem and that if you can reduce or eliminate the 'problems without solutions' reporting, everyone would be much happier and more efficient.

One of the major problems in delegation is the temptation to over-specify the way a task should be performed, rather than letting the subordinate know the objective and giving them a relatively free hand to find the route to it. Similarly, every time someone brings you a problem it is very important that you force yourself to ask for *their* ideas about a solution before volunteering your own. Rushing in with an opinion may have several adverse effects, including:

- distorting their response
- preventing you hearing it at all
- tempting them to bring you future problems without thinking about solutions.

In the recruitment context, keep on asking for opinions before you volunteer yours. Jumping in with both feet may prevent someone else disclosing something relatively minor but significant. You need all the facts you can get – pro and con.

In particular, this principle should improve your chances of identifying your colleagues' prejudices and malpractices, which may well be affecting either their interview performance or their input to the selection process. Keep asking the magic questions, like

'Why?'
'For example?'
'How do you deduce that?'
'What are his good points?'
'Where does she fall short of the specification?'

This will actually be easier than it sounds. The resemblance to an inquisition may not be noticed because most people like the sound of their own voice and their own opinions. You are giving them a chance to gratify that preference.

By now you have lots of data:

- a CV and/or application form for each person
- a candidate specification
- interview notes
- test results
- perhaps some informal references if it has been possible to take these up without damage to the candidates.

Finally you have arrived at the point when you want to (or have to) make a decision.

Decisions, decisions

This is one of the key areas for improvement and your last chance to correct errors made earlier.

For instance, you may need to correct gaps in your data, errors in the candidate specification and wrong-headedness in your colleagues!

On the first point, have you really got enough data to make objective decisions? Your criteria will probably fall naturally into the following categories:

- age: easy, but probably not crucial
- education (secondary): is easily verified too
- degree: easily proved, seldom checked. How important is it? Later qualifications may be more important and, in the author's experience, are more often claimed untruthfully. Check, but also have a last think about their necessity
- experience: may well be crucial and a good CV plus dedicated references may give you comfort. Do not trust interview assessments alone; most bright people can describe the job above or around them unless there is unique technical content. Was there a chance to use work samples?
- health: observe and test. Medical examinations are a good investment and should be more widespread. The key employee who imports a chronic or, at any rate, recurring condition costs a lot in time, money and morale. Even if this was not in your candidate specification it should be implicit and, at the point of selection, perhaps should be a condition of the offer?
- personality, including emotional stability: as for physical health – observe and check
- IQ: important, so have you tested for it?
- application of intelligence: even more important, so test
- aptitudes, attitudes, team behaviour, management style: did you really get *all* these out of the interview? Consider whether you should test

- what have they achieved, changed, improved, prevented, rescued and launched? Does your paperwork cover this fully?
- how would they contribute?

Indecision

It is quite likely that your candidate specifications do not cover the above points to the extent that they should. Bringing them out into the open *and writing them down* for debate avoids the possibility that those participating in the decision have different criteria and different 'facts' against each. Some may be mentally coded 'essential' without being disclosed as such to colleagues! This is quite important because the decision point often involves reviewing the selection criteria again – sometimes in desperation, sometimes because the recruitment process has enhanced your appreciation of the market and the art of the possible.

Best and worst

It will come as no surprise to you that the selection decision often has to be taken in circumstances less than ideal. There are six possibilities, only one of which can be described as ideal:

(a) One person meets the specification and you all want to hire him or her. This is not the ideal, both because you have no choice and because at least one of your colleagues is likely to feel cheated since the decision doesn't 'feel right' unless they've turned down someone else. This, by the way, is one of the consultancy world's pet hates – 'Yes, Smith is fine, but can we have a look at some more . . .' It is the battle cry of the indecisive executive who doesn't realize that the moment you meet the first person who fits the criteria the clock starts ticking and increases the chance of losing that candidate!

If you have done the recruitment exercise properly, the fact that there is only one acceptable candidate tells you something about the supply situation and the relative rarity of the beasts you are hunting. Make an offer.

(b) Alternatively, several meet the specification and you like them all. This is the ideal, in that you have a choice, but it also demands that you look again at the criteria and apply your minds to the relative weight of each. Choice is a luxury but it may mean you stray into subjective or trivial matters. You would do well to steer your colleagues round this potential pitfall, possibly by reviewing whether the quality of the candidates matches your needs, not by introducing extra agendas.

(c) The next problem may be that one or more candidates meet the specification but you don't want to hire them. Go back to the drawing board. Are you implying criteria which you have not codified? Do you have qualitative standards which are higher than those listed? Or is somebody making subjective judgements which you should not introduce into the process? Worse, are they objective judgements on matters not capable of being incorporated into the conventional specification? Not illegal ones, but perhaps an intuitive assessment, based on bitter experience. For example, do the negative factors in a candidate's record suggest that he is a con-man? Insurers look to their claims experience. Managers look to their bitter practical experience.

We are treading on difficult ground here. The author is aware that iron discipline is necessary if we are not to fall over the edge into a morass of subjectivity, but there are respectable precedents. The person who always has a good reason for leaving jobs at two-year intervals is almost certain to have an equally good reason for leaving you, before the task is done . . . Similarly it usually takes two to make a personality clash, even if the blame is on a 9:1 basis. You may well feel that your environment is so good and supportive that it will cure all the malcontents and malingerers. Congratulations, if it is, but don't hire on that assumption until you have objective historic evidence!

In the meantime, find out *why* you don't feel comfortable about the hiring. Don't just dismiss the candidate. There may well be a valid reason, but you need the reason before you can make the decision. Rejection without that analysis may result in your losing the perfect candidate to a competitor who is less subjective.

(d) The same qualitative analysis applies in reverse: when nobody meets the specification but you want to hire someone who doesn't. This may tell you more about the specification. It is in fact the acid test of the specification, always providing that you can arrive at an objective reason for revising it. If not, recognize what shortfall you might be accepting. You may be amused to know that this is the reason why consultants and agencies often put up a 'joker', who does not fully meet the specification but, in their view, could do the job. This is the

The Joker

perfect way of making the pragmatic client recognize that the specification might have been too tight. When a degree is 'essential', but the real requirement is for someone *able* to get into university but who has chosen not to, or could not afford to, the other bits of the specification suddenly become more important. This is an opportunity, not a problem.

(e) The penultimate situation is that there are no candidates who meet the specification and none for whom you would bend it. Nevertheless, look again at the one who comes nearest and review how well he or she would do the job. There is no point in starting the exercise again if the same result is likely. Look at the possibility of changing the job to fit the best candidate. Look again at the internal people in the light of your better knowledge of the market. You now know more about the problem. Don't ignore that bonus.

(f) Finally, you may have no candidates, in spite of all the money and effort you have expended. Don't start again. Learn from the failure. Review internal solutions. Take counsel about the viability of the specification and your sourcing decisions. If you must do it again, find ways to do it better!

Invidious Comparisons

There is another tool which you can use in the selection process, not as a final decider, but as a significant filter. In brief, where have they been? At managerial level and to a lesser extent at support levels, people's track record can be a particularly good indicator of general merit. The difficulty is that you are going to have to build up your own data bank of examples – although in your own sector, and sometimes function, you may have some ideas already. Start codifying them. Start asking candidates and colleagues. You will soon get a picture of the outfits (usually, but not always, big) where somebody's presence at a specific period tells you something about them. This is not the same as assuming that so-and-so is an IBM, ICI or Unilever 'type'. (This is different and applies to long-service people, if at all.)

What we are looking for are the companies where the quality and style of hiring, development and retention in a specific period was such that you can deduce one of the following:

- merely being hired by that company is a good sign, or
- hiring plus survival for a reasonable period is an acceptable indicator
- anyone who got accelerated development in all or a known part of the company must be good news
- anyone who was fired by the, usually idiosyncratic, chief executive, is likely to be assertive and of high moral tone (if that's what you want)

None of these is an absolute indicator but as you build up your evidence you will be pleasantly surprised how often you are right. Consider using this earlier in the process as a pre-interview filter as well.

Offer and Acceptance

Recruiters speak of offers. Lawyers speak of offer and acceptance. We would do well to emulate them. There is a tendency amongst weathered recruiters to issue an offer as a last desperate gesture at the end of a recruitment exercise, then lie back and pray because a substantial minority of offers do not get accepted. This is not good enough. And improvement is possible. There are several areas where you can ensure better practice and thus better results. You deserve them, because you are, at last, communicating with someone you want for the organization after all those hours and weeks dealing with people who won't quite fit.

Offers can be better. They can be:

- quicker
- warmer
- better researched
- better packaged
- better explained
- easier to accept.

It is very unlikely that all the offers emanating from your organization are perfect. Sharpening up practice on this point can, by itself, have a magical effect on your success in recruitment. Add it to improvements in the other areas discussed, and it becomes the icing on the cake.

Speed should be automatic, but often is not. If you delegate the task of preparing the offer to anyone who is less interested, the chances of delay increase. Your own team may know that something which has to go out on a Friday, must do so – and by the midday post – if it is to stand a chance of arriving on Saturday. Alas, the company system may force you to have it issued by another section, which doesn't regard deadlines in quite the same light: the offer isn't finally approved until Monday, misses Monday night's post because nobody cares too much and, by the way, goes out second-class because there's an economy drive on.

Any one of these loses you the chance of having the candidate consider the offer peacefully over the weekend. Put together, they can make you look slipshod and uninterested.

This is not just a question of competing with some other bidder. You can lose out to the present employer, or be rejected even if there is no other bidder and the candidate is unemployed.

Candidates are both proud and thoughtful. Warmer offers help to convince them. This means more than ending with a brief phrase about looking forward to working with them. The phraseology of the letter should be constructive, not a mass of constraints. Don't write legalistic offers. Save that for the formal contract if corporate policy forces you to 'do the heavy'.

Remember that candidates may be holding another offer – identical in content – with only the quality of your prose to tip the scales! Better research at interview would probably have warned you about the other imminent offer(s). It would also have enabled you to ascertain several key points:

- the true value and precise detail of the candidate's present rewards
- the range in which an acceptable future package might lie. Always ask for a range, not a cold single figure, for instance: 'There must be two salary figures you have in mind: the base, if all other conditions are perfect, and another at which you'd feel overpaid or begin to worry if it included danger money'. Use your own phrases, but force them to think about the matter and disclose
- whether salary actually matters – this flows naturally from the previous enquiry. In some situations, parity with existing or past salary is more than adequate and other factors like security or prospects are paramount. Alternatively, at the other end of the scale a candidate may, quite rightly, expect a massive uplift to market rate because of a recent qualification or unique slice of experience. In between, a conventional, perhaps modest, increment will suffice. Without research you don't know in which area you are.

Better packaging means more than warm words. It should go without saying that the offer must look good, be complete and devoid of error (although some of the author's clients still haven't managed to implement this philosophy) but you could surround it with trimmings which make it more tempting. If the

Warmer offers help to convince them

company car is, say, a Skoda Rapid, enclose the brochure on the beast and its rally record, provide photographs of the company house, the leaflet on the sports facilities or the chatty booklet about pensions, for older candidates! You must have *something* special. Flaunt it.

Better explanations follow naturally. It may be in your mind to give an early review in order to get over corporate constraints about maximum hiring points in the salary grade. This could be presented in one of four ways, as follows:

- you omit to mention salary reviews at all
- you specify the next review date (and the pessimistic candidates wonder whether they will be eligible for review so soon, or whether the review will be worthwhile)
- you specify the next review date and make it clear that, because you think highly of their potential, you are going to arrange a generous review. This is less of a trap than it seems, because if they are useless you may well want to terminate them instead – not ideal, but do not forget the existence of the option
- all the promises and forecasts made at the various interviews need to be mentioned and codified in the offer letter. Omitting them makes the candidate think you have forgotten them, so you don't get value from them. Worse, if you don't mention them in the text, you, or your successor, probably *will* forget them, thereby thoroughly damaging the candidate's morale. *Explain* how unusual benefits are going to work to avoid similar damage.

How can you ensure more acceptable offers? There are three key ways in which this can be achieved – and you can probably invent others.

First, the face to face, 'How would you feel if we put together an offer like this . . .' approach can smooth the path for the later text. If the buying signals are very obvious, have the text run off while the meeting is still going on (what are word processors for, after all?). Second, if the offer has to be made by letter, invite a telephone call as a preliminary acceptance, or a chance to discuss on the phone anything that is unclear (don't say 'unacceptable' or you may create negotiation where none was needed). Third, make it easy for them to reply. A reply-paid (first-class) envelope and duplicate of the offer to sign should help – or show willingness to accept a fax! Alternatively, you could hand deliver the offer and invite them to use your courier later, at your expense, to return the acceptance. Packaging again!

It may seem a bit overdone, but if you are pitching for a top operator in an outgoing function such as sales, promotions, PR, etc, do consider whether an otherwise gross gesture might not tip the scales. Perhaps:

- a bottle of champagne with the offer
- the offer delivered by a security firm
- a singing delivery . . .
- the keys to the new and very nice company car (but cut more spares before you let them go)

Gross, as I have said, but you've met the candidate, I have not. You may have more relevant ideas – but don't try them on actuaries and security staff!

The offer and the acceptance can come together more often. The offer is the first step in the induction programme, so you could include sending copies of the press release about the new venture they're going to be involved in, as part of the offer package. This applies equally to accountants, PR people, secretaries and welders. They're all susceptible to up-market flattery – or packaging, as we call it.

Don't under-rate the power of the press release. At senior level you should put key people on the distribution list during the period between offer and joining. Not only is it good communications policy, it reduces the risk they'll read something that surprises them in the press and withdraw that precious acceptance. Lots of acceptances get withdrawn. That is why the induction process has to start *immediately,* both mechanically and on a personal level. The period after the candidate has accepted an offer, but before joining, is a very lonely time when all the doubts creep in. Family, friends and ex-employers work on those doubts. Fight back, even if you don't know who the enemy is!

Fight back, even if you don't know who
the enemy is

Induction

Induction is a deceptive part of the recruitment process. On the one hand it may appear to be outside the recruitment area, on the other, its proper performance is crucial to the successful outcome. There are several good books on induction, one of them published by the IPM – *Getting Off to a Good Start* by Alan Fowler. We cannot improve on that here, but a few thoughts may be helpful.

First, the induction process starts at your first meeting with the successful candidate. It is important that all promises and forecasts made to the candidate are recorded, not just so that the offer document can be comprehensive but so that you know what you have to live up to later. That record should be studied again before the candidate arrives, and at each periodic review. It is unproductive to appraise people without recognizing that they are also appraising your corporate performance. The candidate is much more likely to note and remember broken promises, than the company is to recall the 'promise' perceived in the candidate's performance at interview.

Second, recognizing that the induction programme extends from offer to the point of joining, helps you to keep the candidates warm in that period. It may be the time at which they are most excited about the prospect of joining and most willing to:

- read preparatory material
- welcome corporate press releases
- undergo light training or familiarization

At the very least, find excuses for keeping in touch with them. The battle is not yet won and, in spite of the acceptance you hold, if they are any good at all their current employers are fighting a rearguard action and the employers whom you pipped at the post are considering how to get the decision reversed. This may seem like gazumping. It is. And there is no ethical code to inhibit past or potential employers from doing their best to upset the deal. Keeping in touch with the candidates so that they remember your merits must be a good investment.

. . . their current employers are fighting
a rearguard action

For the mechanical process of induction, no outsider can produce a comprehensive list of recommendations about the way you run people in, but it is important that you do just that. Produce a formal list, of which everyone involved in the induction process is aware, not least so that everything on it gets done and you do not demotivate the candidate by omissions or boring repetitions.

Consider also whether some of the briefing could be on video. By definition you were short staffed until the new arrival and that situation remains until he or she is fully operational. Diluting the induction burden may smooth the transition. So does sharing the load, via a structured programme. Briefing by several people is a better introduction than a hurried handshake in the corridor and a forgotten name, repeated several times.

There is one hangover from the interview which may not appear on an internal checklist. Keep asking questions and listening to everything the novice says. Misunderstandings and misconceptions can be identified and corrected. It may even be the last chance to correct some of them, because some will merely vanish into background memory and be recalled as part of the house culture. Others, if gross, will cause early resignation!

Finally, don't regard the induction period as an alternative to work. Instead, it is the most sensitive time for instilling good work practices, under supervision and by example. Working flat out on something worthwhile sets the tone.

THE EMPLOYERS' VIEW

The Employers' View

Most of this book has been the author's distillation of facts, or his opinions, obtained during a period largely filled with selection consulting experience. This, although it qualifies him as a professional recruiter, is no substitute for the successful experience of people in industry and commerce who recruit for their own teams.

The notes which follow come from a diverse collection of functional heads and general managers who depend on good people. In general they reinforce the message of the rest of the book but there are several new ideas, some disagreements and one or two heresies!

Incidentally, some of them, although not personnel specialists or full-time recruiters, may be very professional about their recruitment efforts. Recruitment, after all, is probably not a profession. I am indebted to Berry Wilson, former personnel director of British Leyland and now a headhunter, for his observation that recruitment is, at best, in line with Hans Keller's definition of a phoney profession. It certainly meets the three key criteria set out in his book *Criticism* (Faber and Faber) as follows:

Phoney professions have to
- be highly respected, even admired, within their civilization or at least that part of it affected by their activities
- create grave problems which they then fail to solve
- and have a capacity to criticize somebody or something negatively and self-righteously with aplomb.

It follows that recruitment, if a profession, is only a phoney one. Berry Wilson suggests that we should be content for it to be regarded as a trade – albeit a craft trade.

The comments which follow are, therefore, from members of other professions who sometimes practise the 'craft' of recruitment, for profit.

We noted with interest that two contributors practise management well enough to delegate the task of replying to subordinates!

Ted Simpson, of outplacement specialists Sanders and Sidney, offers a glimpse of how they recruit:

> '1. Happily, we have never had to "recruit" consultants. Applications come in in such numbers that it becomes a selection process. We, therefore, have a pretty good idea that people are interested in the position before they come along. This doesn't mean they are all good. Hopefully, it means they are all interested.
> 2. We have fairly tight job specifications covering what we expect of consultants. It applies both to full-time and part-time. We try not to give way on these principles no matter how persuasive a candidate might be.
> 3. Applications for positions are circulated around our Board for approval before the candidate comes in. Unless we all feel quite strongly about the candidate, he or she doesn't come in.
> 4. We ask for, and check, references, looking particularly at the reason they would be interested in leaving their last employ to get into outplacement and/or to join us.
> 5. We try not to over recruit – difficult because we never know when peaks and valleys will occur. It's unsatisfactory to recruit staff on a full-time basis if you haven't enough work to go around. It's also difficult to keep part-timers happy if they don't have assignments. We try to have too few rather than too many. Over recruiting can create rather an unpleasant problem.
> 6. When we have enough work to require a new full-timer we try to elevate a part-timer into the position. That way we know how they will perform, have a view of their track record, before we add them to our permanent staff.'

Barrie Pearson, of Livingstone Fisher Associates, known to many for his long association with Ashridge, was brief:

> '● emphasize the match of chemistry when recruiting
> ● look for tangible evidence of an achiever
> ● select people over at least three separate meetings
> ● induct people by working on a project with an established manager to underline common standards.'

Robert Clinton, of Greig Middleton corporate finance, has been in lots of big structured environments with big recruitment teams, but now admits to a more traditional resource (interesting to know it is still feasible . . .):

'The way that I and my colleagues recruit at Greig Middleton is, in the main, the way that stockbrokers have recruited for the last hundred years or so – ie sons of friends and, on occasions, daughters. Strangely, this does actually work although we do, of course, have the odd failure. Most of the people who are brought into the firm are brought in relatively young, trained on the job and paid a pittance. We find that there is almost an endless supply of really good, keen, young people willing and anxious to work. This may, I think, have a certain amount to do with the philosophy and outlook of the firm, but I am sure that there are others that have the same experience.'

Eric Frye, probably best known as joint managing director of Plessey in the 1970s and from the Ford finance team of the 1960s, now retired, feels:

'there is no substitute for the lessons of experience but few are lucky enough to have the experience before they have to face the task or the problems. This is an attempt to pass on a little of that experience! I have learned to:

- avoid double firsts, particularly from Oxbridge. Many have failed completely; only one successfully adjusted to industry – brilliant treasurer but still with some communication problems
- trust one's own judgement – important for those who work for you
- only listen to your superiors if they have really a good record in recruitment – except for hiring me, most of mine have not!
- first impressions are important – subsequent knowledge has varied but never contradicted them
- use recruitment specialists – don't let them use you
- current position and remuneration are very unreliable guides: how many people do you know who have jobs where either they or their jobs are overrated? They have been put out to grass or demoted sideways, or even upwards
- don't hesitate to terminate a square peg: both he/she and you will be better off. I have even been thanked by the people concerned.'

Donald MacKeith, financial director of Land Securities, offers the following notes on hiring, using and developing people:

'Most of the appointments which have been long lasting have been people of whom I had prior experience, through their having been engaged on audit and accountancy work for the company. This cuts down the lead-in time and "getting to know" period but is not without drawbacks. By engaging the modern accountant straight out of a professional office one gets a product with a blinkered approach to his role, who lives by his job specification, has an intolerant attitude to other disciplines and an ignorance of practical corporate decision-making.

The latter all leads to much counselling, but this itself strengthens the personal relationship and raises it above a purely master/servant one.

I tend to take on the ambitious although I know it makes my life more uncomfortable. I encourage them to broaden themselves both by courses and outside contacts.'

Malcom Hart, sales and marketing director of Rolls Royce Motor Cars Ltd makes a pertinent point about consistently poor performers:

'If senior managers fail to grasp the nettle and fire such people, then there is almost inevitably a backlash with the remainder of the workforce which results in demoralization or demotivation. Other employees seeing this kind of thing going on either feel that they can do the same or, perhaps worse, resent management for not acting decisively – either way it is bad news.'

Carol Friend, managing director of Pielle PR comments:

'We have made our mistakes in taking on one or two people who are excellent interviewees but lousy operators and who give one opinion (eg no problem in working/reporting to a woman) but demonstrate the reverse once employed. Our recruitment success over the past four years demonstrates that we have learned our lessons and now apply the following:

- always see likely candidates on a "career advice" basis to provide a recruitment database for the future

- initial fact finding interview – one key interviewer with a second person participating if the candidate looks likely after the first twenty minutes
- second meeting preferably led by the second person above and possibly with a third senior staff member to take another view
- give the executives with whom the candidate will be working the chance to meet and talk with them to give their opinion.'

She cites a relevant example:

'Two good candidates: chairman chose one; operating director determined "fitting in" was the only thing to choose between them; executives chose opposite to chairman because his choice "would not cope with the pace". The selected candidate was a real winner.'

Peter Cole of Melrose Film Productions believes that good recruitment is the key to business success.

'If people are right, *everything* else flows from it.

I make recruiting a personal priority. I don't use search etc because I feel that the people I am interested in are out of mainstream. Running the whole process from scratch is immensely time consuming, but it seems to me inescapable. Having made the decision that we must do it ourselves, it follows that *I* must do it myself. This may well be inefficient and overkill, but it is a *personal* commitment which I feel is the basis of our whole business success – my way of saying there is nothing more important.'

John Leighfield, chairman and chief executive of Istel Ltd, describes a few tactics that have been employed to strengthen their recruitment:

- ' the use of a "bounty" scheme whereby members of our staff do their own head-hunting to bring their friends in similar jobs in other companies into our company. The sums of money (typically £500) are worthwhile to the bounty hunter, but trivial compared with normal recruitment costs. The people recruited tend to be local, which means that they are naturally more loyal, of high calibre (because our people do not want to be seen to bring in inadequate performers) and are immediately at home.

- making use of personal contacts back into companies from whom we have recruited individuals. We have been successful in using one recruit to drag behind him a whole series of others. Quite often, this has had the double effect of again being very cost-effective recruitment together with strengthening us (because they tend to bring in the better people) and weakening a competitor (because that is where we tend to recruit from)
- deliberately targeting the good people that we see in competitive organizations.'

Derek Bell-Jones, managing director of Deeko plc has one practical idea:

'When you get your top four people in for second interviews by the manager, which may be in line with the first interview by the managing director, have a thirty-minute "test" for them, which they each sit under similar conditions. That shows in words and deeds rather than by verbal communication whether they have knowledge of the subject. If they are a purchasing manager, say, questions can be set about preferred suppliers under certain conditions, and they have to think through their answers.

It is then often interesting to get four answers independently marked by a couple of senior executives rather than by the interviewer who may be biased by the personal assessment he has made.

This is by no means a panacea, it is often information that can add to making the right decision for the right executive.'

Bob Nellist confesses that during his long experience in major groups, he could have:

- taken more time and care over the entire recruitment process. It is the single most important activity to claim my time and attention at work
- been more persistent when my initial recruitment efforts met with failure
- promoted from within more boldly. This has seldom disappointed me. When it has failed me I have always had the compensation that at least I tried
- been more ambitious in the standards I have set for job candidates. There are lots of good people out there

looking for a boss like me. I have all too frequently been too idle or insufficiently persistent to find them
- used more fully all available tests; in spite of the fact that my use of consultant psychologists led me into as many spectacular recruitment cock-ups as I did, more cheaply, without their assistance.'

Sheila McAuley, managing director of British Airways Enterprises, includes the following key factors:

'• recruit people of high energy, enthusiasm and good commitment to a job which is two levels above them and let them grow into the job
- give people space to grow, take risks and make some mistakes. Good people always learn much more than the mistake really costs
- a mix of these two is ideal.'

David Say, of James Hardie Industries, has a pragmatic view.

'The best (and possibly only satisfactory) head-hunting that I have done has been without the services of a recognized head-hunter. I have asked friends and colleagues, "Do you know of a chap" (as an Aussie, I consider 'chap' to be a non-sexist word) "to fill such-and-such position?" Or, "Do you know of anybody in XYZ Limited which has just been taken over by those Pommy Bastards, ABC plc?" If the answer is "yes", and it often is if you ask in the right circles, you have the advantage of:

- getting someone known to people you know and trust (and perhaps I should be more trusting of my head-hunting acquaintances)
- getting someone who really wants to move (candidate targets are too easily seduced by the head-hunter into "winning-the-interview" games and often don't seriously consider moving until they are actually offered the job)
- it's a damn sight cheaper!'

Stephen Warshaw, managing director of Hutchinson Press Ltd, suggests:

'• writing exciting ads
- being prepared to recruit outside the obvious type of candidate (but very selectively)

- a tendency to look for people similar to one's own image of oneself (can be dangerous!)
- promoting from within
- recruiting people who will challenge me, question, and probe (ie not "yes" men and women)
- getting the best people one can possibly find, but always remembering that second best may well be good enough in some circumstances. For example, there aren't many first-class expatriates in Japan!
- not being afraid to approach the person I want direct
- interviewing everyone *at least* twice (the time is always worth it and the change of opinion can be dramatic)
- if possible, involving people in the interviewing process that are going to be working with the interviewee
- I try to give a relevant "written task" to every candidate at every level for every type of job
- spending as much time letting people interview you and "the company" as you spend interviewing them
- trust written references even less than verbal ones!
- try to get opinions from people who are *not* given as referees
- don't rush recruitment. Whenever I have been under pressure to appoint a person I am not sure of, I have almost always been wrong.'

David Probert, chairman of W Canning plc comments briefly:

'I look for energy, enthusiasm, entrepreneurial ability, track record and integrity, in reverse order. I understand from the history books that if Monty had a vacancy for a general, he looked for the glint of battle in the candidates' eyes and I have some sympathy with this.'

THE PROFIT EFFECT

The Profit Effect

The first part of this book has been about the ways you can make recruitment more cost-effective. We have, therefore, now covered:

less recruitment	hiring people who stay
	hiring fewer people to replace the mediocre
cheaper recruitment:	cheaper and free sources
	better, cost-effective processing
	getting good people before your competitors do
best practice	avoiding delay, chiselling, prevarication etc
	selecting better.

The next slice is about the ways better recruitment can make the organization more profitable, beyond the economies implicit in the above.

The opportunities are massive. If the programme described is fully implemented it offers you:

- more time for other things
- better performance
- better profits

and improved morale, working relationships and attitudes, all of which should have a positive effect on the way the corporate machine works.

This cannot all be achieved overnight, but some of the benefits are immediate and some obtainable before their cause has been fully implemented. For instance, many of the benefits will flow from employees' perception of what the organization is trying to do, so that you will get some credit for the future effects. You may also keep people you would otherwise have lost and/or be able to allocate people to the future structure and jobs, even if that structure is not quite ready. Reasonable people (of whom you should have a better supply) will tolerate much if there is light at the end of the tunnel!

Can Improving People Improve Profits?

The official answer (without which this book would not exist) is in the affirmative but it is important that we justify the answer; not least because there are several other possible answers which may spring to mind, like 'No' or 'some people are beyond improvement', and cynicism in general about the link between improvements and profits.

This leads naturally to the question 'can we improve people at all?' Only a cynic or a defeatist would answer *'No'* but there are two caveats. Some people may not be worth much investment of time and money because they are not bright enough to be transformed. Some managers, in the hurly-burly of running a company, feel they cannot find time to improve themselves and others. These managers need to be reassured that there *is* a dividend and that time spent on good training is repaid – as long as the beneficiaries are not totally useless. In principle, every hour of training should repay the organization if it does one or more of the following:

- it enables managers to delegate more
- it avoids gratuitous errors
- it produces qualitative and perhaps quantitative improvements in output
- it reduces the need for supervision, and thus
- it saves management time

Reminding management of these benefits is a constant problem. As with the classic progression in selling, from

unawareness → awareness and comprehension → decision and action

The reverse process, regressing towards unawareness, also exists. Managers forget – or they remember only when reminded – because the training need is not uppermost in their minds. Most long-lead problems and opportunities are pushed out of the way when those with short fuses are visible.

Can Improving People Improve Profits?

The ideal solution is full-time training but the cost and disruption is prohibitive in most cases. What we need, to prove that people can improve on the job, is a pragmatic and cost-effective approach which gets over the 'management theory doesn't apply to my bit of the business' attitude. Training, like management theory, must be seen to be *practical* before it is practised.

The objective itself is eminently practical. It is better profitability. To identify how we can improve people in this direction we need to review the ways they can improve profits. The crudest split might be:

- lower expenses, with same revenues
- higher revenues, with same expenses
- better margins, as revenues and expenses increase.

There is a fourth possibility, that profits are maintained while revenues reduce, but this is rare and hard to achieve unless the overhead element is low to start with.

Nearly all of these can be helped by good recruitment coupled to a relevant training and development programme. The latter is the key. Good recruitment alone is not enough if the benefits are to be fully enjoyed. The following sections will cover some of the ways planned recruitment and people improvement can influence the profit and loss account, directly or through reducing the capital employed. Examples include:

- less people
- more efficient structures
- better returns on training
- better routes to corporate objectives
- bringing the worst performers up to the norm, and the average performers above it
- 'zero-fault' performance – the direct and indirect benefits
- how equal opportunity policies can improve profits
- recruiting people who can train others.

None of these are particularly difficult, except the obligation to keep on remembering to implement the necessary quality controls and filters, and the follow-through.

Reliability

Regrettably, a lot of management time is spent monitoring how other managers, supervisors and the serried ranks below them, do their work. Much of this burden is unnecessary and can be reduced or eliminated by proper recruitment and training. Perhaps the greatest single bonus of good recruitment and training is the potential for reliable work performance. This can mean less time wasted, more time applied to constructive tasks and, properly planned, less managerial staff. The benefits are massive. Reliability is the key. Quite apart from time saved on monitoring and correcting, quality assurance benefits every aspect of work, for example:

- goods and services are always received by customers on time
- incoming supplies are ordered to arrive (just) in time
- internal and external correspondence, reports, etc are always on time
- other tasks are performed when planned, or the people affected are made aware of both the revised timing and the reason
- invoices, statements and chasing procedures always happen promptly, so
- monies due to the organization flow in promptly
- people's rewards and benefits reach them without demotivating delays and haggles.

If you are already running an organization like this, congratulations. If not, there is room for improvement. But how? Some of it comes from making sure that people know what their responsibilities and priorities are. But this will not help if you are trying to train people who are not right for the jobs in the first place.

Tests, reference-checking and work samples can enable you to be more objective and to answer very specific questions about potential employees, or those you want to switch around. For example:

Regrettably, a lot of management time is spent
monitoring other managers

'This man is less intelligent than the people whose current performance is barely acceptable. Can we tolerate worse performance?'

'This woman has a very low anxiety level on her 16PF, which, in conjunction with other indicators, suggests she will not give enough attention to deadlines or customer and peer group needs. Do we really need that sort of behaviour?'

'His references suggest poor timekeeping. Can the security function afford the risk that he won't be there at a crucial changeover'?

'The work sample (in-basket exercise) makes it very clear that she doesn't understand the priorities of the job. Yet she's bright. Shall we take the risk that we can train her to prioritize better?'

Of course the questions are loaded. Some may not be so clearcut, but if you do not give yourself the chance to ask them, using the authoritative data available, you hire a 'time bomb'. Substandard performers don't just need more management, they need correction time and even then they demotivate the people around them. If you surround good but non-assertive people with mediocre ones, the ones who will leave will be the best . . .

Check what your existing good people are really like and try hard to recruit more of them, by using every legal filter in your selection 'shopping basket'. There's gold dust to be found.

Incidentally, do not be seduced by the author's mention of a low level on the anxiety line of a 16PF into assuming that a high anxiety score is necessarily the magic solution to the selection of reliable people. The author talked both to Dr Andrew Stewart of Informed Choice and Dr Ken Miller of the Independent Assessment and Research Centre about relevant tests for this trait. The recommendation is that the 16PF and the more recent Savile and Holdsworth equivalent are both appropriate but your adviser is likely to be looking at a combination of factors rather than a raw score on anxiety.

Andrew Stewart also feels that the Myers Briggs test offers a more positive indicator, with ISTJ (Introverted Sensing Thinking Judging) types being the epitome of reliability. ESTJs are also above average in this area. Fortunately, there are a lot of STJ types around so the quest for reliability permits you to look at a substantial minority of the population.

Alas, if you also want high intelligence there is some evidence that NTJs (N stands for Intuitive, by the way) – the entrepreneurs – have a somewhat better share of the high IQ population. Reliable they may not be. It is no accident that Dr Ischak Adizes uses the word 'arsonist' to describe people with well-developed, perhaps over-developed, entrepreneurial characteristics. The arsonist lights fires for other people to tend or put out.

Don't be put off the NTJs. You may need some, but an excess of them can be very wearing. A balanced team is the ideal, with a large slab of 'old reliables' to depend on.

Do not be put off by the 'old'. Perhaps old-fashioned maturity would be a better description since these people come in all shapes, sizes and ages. They may be your youngest employees, they may be the oldest. What you can be sure of is that they understand what they are doing, or ask if they do not, and plough competently on doing it in the right way with few or no errors. In the sales area they bring home orders, not excuses. Accounts appear on time and correct. The reliable support staff tend to finish things before they go sick or take time off for other reasons.

This may all sound terribly basic but if you compare and contrast the positive impact of these people against the negative impact of those who don't meet these standards, whose work and behaviour demands a significant level of management attention because you have to sweep up after them, mollify those around them, make excuses for them to suppliers and customers, correct their grosser errors and then find someone to stand in for them when they are unexpectedly absent (getting a new job, one hopes), the opportunity becomes clearer.

Unfortunately it is all too easy to tolerate the mildly unreliable rather than face the nuisance of firing and re-hiring. Given a small dose of apathy, the problem can be tolerated for months or years. It is your decision, but do bear the possible benefits in mind.

There is also a middle ground. Sometimes the employees around the unreliable specimen, the ones who have been 'carrying' the offender, will actually perform better and more productively with nobody in the job for a while if the matter is properly explained to them. In extreme cases you may find that the job does not exist or does exist but is being performed by people other than the apparent job holder.

109

Reliable support staff tend to finish things before
they go sick or take time off for other reasons

This neatly exemplifies one route to the earlier objective of 'same result from less people'. If the job really does need to be done full-time, hire a better performer – a reliable one, and you move on to the second acceptable objective 'same number of people, better results'.

One useful bonus, if there is a lull between the old and new incumbents, is the chance to find out what the job really *is*. Someone, beside, above or below the job, should do it for a short period with the brief, not just to keep the job going, but to record what it really consists of.

There will be several prior interpretations, not all of them on record, including:

- the agreed job description
- what the previous job holder understood by it
- what the previous job holder was actually doing
- what everyone else assumed was being done.

The advantage of a review during the interregnum is that it may become apparent how the job could be improved, expanded, simplified or brought into line with the ideal implicit in the original job description or with the peer group assumption about the true purpose of the job!

Failure to take advantage of this break is a common omission, but it only takes a few minutes each day to codify what has to be done and the benefits are massive.

It may even be that a job description revised under these pressures gives a clearer picture of the priorities within the job than the usual routine exercise performed on related jobs as if on an assembly line.

This leads naturally to one of the author's favourite techniques: plagiarizing the techniques of other functions. In this instance, 'Value Analysis' comes to mind. Its use in a manufacturing design environment is well known. The engineers look at a component and try to identify what simpler, cheaper equivalent could perform the required function as well as, or better than, the existing item. So it can be with jobs and with each task within a job. Put on your engineer's hat and think through each part of the job, asking:

- could it be done better?
- could it be done more simply?
- does it all need to be done?
- does it need to be done at all?

The results of this process may not translate directly into profit but there is a fairly close connection. The primary objective here is not a headcount reduction exercise, although that opportunity may be one of the results, but a genuine attempt to clean up the quality and value of each job studied. The headcount reduction is, in this instance, icing on the cake. But what icing! Never forget the advantages – substantial or peripheral – such as:

- the reduction in semi-variable overheads (people generate substantial cost by being there, quite apart from the space they occupy)
- a reduction in idle time: gossip, in case you hadn't noticed, increases as the square of the number of people in a group
- less people generally need less supervision
- two half people (not necessarily job-sharing) tend to do more work than a single whole one.

The value analysis programme may also permit de-skilling, so the job can be filled by someone cheaper, or easier to find in a skills shortage.

The final benefit brings us back to the reliability theme. If the value analysis programme cleans up the job, it should result in a more efficient and satisfactory job content. This, coupled with the selection of people who are innately predisposed to doing things correctly and promptly, must help to generate a zero-fault attitude and practice. The benefits are manifold:

- no wastage of product or time
- no complaints
- reduced warranty costs and/or extended warranties
- increased customer goodwill
- increased re-purchase rate
- reduction in quality control staff and related costs.

Some of this spells reduced costs. The rest implies increased revenues. Both are attractive: the latter is exciting but do not forget that the former is most effective since a 'free' cost reduction goes straight to the bottom line of the profit and loss account as pure profit! It follows that 10p saved may be equal to 50p or 100p in extra sales.

This is a good reason for having employees who are cost-conscious. Those who, within reason, husband the organiza-tion's resources as if they were their own hard-earned pennies can have a substantial cumulative effect. Contrast the status-conscious executive who feels he or she has a divine right to travel first-class with the one who knows that second-class is equally reliable; the difference in cost is massive. You cannot get discounted tickets (day returns and 'savers') on the first-class scale, so the premium for travelling first is not the apparent 50 per cent which the status-conscious manage to justify to themselves, but, in some cases, more than 100 per cent. You may wonder how on earth this is going to emerge by test or interview. Indicate that their travel expense claim will be at public transport rates and note what they claim . . .

Demographic Time Bomb

Most people are now aware that the number of school leavers in the UK fell in the period 1986-9 and will fall further in the period 1990-5. This general information, however, came as a surprise to many although the relevant data has, by definition, been available for over a decade.

The usual assumption is that this will create a shortage of people available for employment in the 1990s. This is partly true, but the real problem may be different. Shortages imply a gap between supply and demand. Even if the shortfall in supply is not as great as feared, it may well be that increased demand presents an even greater problem in certain functions.

First, let us be clearer about the supply aspect. The shortfall is not evenly distributed across the country or by social class. The geographical imbalance favours the South East; in other words, the fall is less there. Similarly, the fall in supply is significantly less in higher social classes so that if anything, the problem will affect 'blue collar' jobs more than, for instance, graduate recruitment.

This may be no consolation to those already suffering skills shortages but it does offer the chance of damage limitation. Closer study of the patterns in your own organization may suggest that the problem is tolerable or non-existent (except to the extent that future increases in demand will exacerbate the situation). The basic message is, therefore, 'don't panic' because most organizations, unless heavily dependent on skills already in short supply, can improve their recruitment and employment practices to compensate for the true problem.

This requires a 'shopping basket' approach, which can include:

- better, leaner, candidate specifications
- increased mechanization, both at high-tech and intermediate technology levels
- avoidance of discrimination in hiring
- eliminating some jobs
- better selection and training

The individual merits of all these are discussed elsewhere in the book.

The Redundant Degree

One of the problems which appears to threaten us in the 90s is a shortage of graduates. As you can deduce from the previous chapter, this is not necessarily true, but if we go along with the possibility and think what can be done to circumvent it, additional benefits may arise.

The way organizations currently use graduates offers massive encouragement for anyone planning a better recruitment programme. Specifically, the majority of graduates are slotted into jobs where the content of their degree studies is irrelevant to the job or at best peripheral. The fact that *any* graduate can be considered for most functions of management leads us to believe that most people with good 'A' Level results could be used equally well.

What are we looking for:

- intelligence and its application?
- acceptable personality?
- interest in the job?
- keyboard skills?
- reliability?
- good value?

We might also add

- gratitude?

These characteristics are just as likely to be found in school leavers as they are in graduates. The school leavers may even be more grateful. A rethink about the real need for people with degrees might demonstrate that the majority of your 'graduate' vacancies can be filled with carefully selected school leavers, to whom you can offer better relative rewards, more relevant training than they would receive at university *and* support during later extra-mural studies for degree or professional qualifications.

You have also enlarged the size of the pool in which you can fish, because the benefit is not confined to shool leavers. It also permits you to look at other slightly (or much) older people who

. . . 'graduate' vacancies can be filled with
carefully selected school leavers

meet the same intellectual and other criteria. It applies to minority groups who have been overtly or covertly neglected by the employment market so this is also an opportunity for redressing the imbalances.

The majority of people in the UK (and possibly the world) have been programmed to be under-achievers and thus fail to fulfil their potential. In many cases it isn't just society in general which discriminates against them but their own families and culture. In consequence there is a vast reservoir of people out there who, if identified, developed and motivated properly, can help solve skills shortage or just make it possible to hire better all-round employees in less specialized jobs.

This is not going to be easy. The quality of the selection processes and the specification exercises which precede these processes will have to be excellent; but the extra value, at more realistic salaries, which results should more than compensate. Equally, the administrative burden of helping the brighter ones to continue their education must not be under-estimated, but it can still be cost effective, particularly if the employees in the programme are cheaper, more loyal and more relevant than the graduates for whom you would otherwise have paid an unnecessary premium. The fact that you create a reputation for being an above-average user of bright people may also help you get the graduates you still need, on more realistic terms – and they may be volunteers. Their friends, the school-leavers you hire, will have three years to tell the undergraduates about you during vacations!

Discrimination

Discrimination is generally held to be a bad thing. Your organization should not be practising it in recruitment on grounds of race, colour, creed, sex or, dare we say it, age. Discrimination, in its dictionary definition, remains allowable on matters of quality. That is what a selection process is all about. However, it is reasonably certain that many recruiters are practising discrimination in the wrong sense in their everyday hirings. Some of these recruiters are probably in your own organization. This is an opportunity which we can probably best consider by paraphrasing the pragmatic little pamphlet *Equal Opportunities for All* issued by the Federation of Recruitment and Employment Services (FRES), the trade association for employment agencies and selection consultancies.

In brief, FRES starts from the principle that many people are ignorant of employment law and even some of those who are aware of it do not recognize that arguments about best practice had any interest for them. Hence the pamphlet, instead of repeating the legal or moral case against discrimination, makes the *practical* and *profitable* case for good practice!

The arguments are easily summarized. Good people are scarce. In some functions or specific jobs they are scarce enough for shrill cries of 'skills shortages' to be raised. As a consequence, salaries go sky-high or you can only obtain the scarce people on contract rather than as permanent employees.

Reasonable employers would like a wider choice of people, at more reasonable salaries. This potential can be realized in part by making sure that nobody in your own organization is practising illegal or unnecessary discrimination against minorities or even majorities. There is a double benefit: if you succeed and the other people against whom you are competing for employees do not, you will have enlarged your potential pool of people *and* have above average success because there are fewer employers fishing in that pool. You can even exercise positive discrimination and demonstrate your concern by using specialist media to underline your equal opportunity policies.

Market forces being what they are, you may also find that the average cost of new hirings becomes a little more sensible if you are not being held to ransom by a few very scarce specialists. Couple this with better internal selection for training and some shortages may evaporate.

The Skills Explosion

Far too much is written about skills shortages. May we consider the possibility that your organization has a potential skills glut, or could create one?

The standard complaint is usually that people with specialist skills are difficult or expensive to hire and their turnover is high. So what? It is entirely possible that the employers who are complaining have specified their needs wrongly in the first place or, even if they have got it right, are ignoring potential talent close at hand.

There are three levels of solution, all explored in more detail elsewhere in the book, but drawn together here as a reminder of one of the most exciting areas for profit improvement – provided that the jobs are necessary in the first place!

The first opportunity is in the candidate specification. In many cases the employer will ask for someone who has virtually done the same job somewhere else. This is unwise for two reasons: few people want to do an identical job again and, in many cases, someone who is stepping up to it will be more dynamic. Equally, the minimum specification should be for someone with the *potential* to do the job, not with total experience.

The second opportunity concerns internal candidates. The moment you accept that the specification relates to qualities other than duplicated experience, there should be several bright people internally who could be trained and who already know how the organization works – a difficult thing to train for!

Thirdly, there is the question of turnover. There is no absolute solution to this, but if you fill the job with someone who is interested in the risk you are taking and grateful for it, you may get some recognition for good behaviour. Better still, if you transfer someone with a record of loyalty and your decision proves right for them, they are more likely to stay than someone over-priced who has only come for the money and is reading job ads as a matter of course in month one.

There is a further bonus to be gained from recycling internal people. The external candidates are putting on their best face. Their defects are carefully hidden, whereas you know the weaknesses and innate strengths of the internal candidates. And you can test for the things not evident in the previous jobs. Nobody has done everything before, so everyone must have hidden talents: finding them is the key to development.

Human asset accounting died because, legally, people are not assets – and they are often liabilities

Cut Out the Middleperson

Apologies to those of you who recoil from the semantic distortion of the heading, but middlemen would be doubly wrong because, initially, the people being cut out are likely to be women. However, as the principle evolves, both sexes will be eliminated in the process of discarding certain unnecessary jobs. The principle is not new. Mechanization has made it possible to eliminate a lot of jobs, in production, around computers and in the conventional office, over a period of many years. What may come as a surprise is that there is still massive scope for improvement. Only you can decide the particular opportunities in your own organization but I can almost guarantee that there is some wastage around which won't be shaken out without a cynical eye and sanctions.

The principle is simple. You ask which jobs add little, or nothing involving thought or unique skill in the process of carrying out someone else's instructions. You then ask if modern technology could bridge the gap. The answer is usually 'Yes, at a price'. Fortunately that 'price' is disappearing as new technology becomes less new and market forces take effect.

Shorthand is one example. There is very little justification for shorthand, and there has not been for many years, ever since audio recording became available. The dictaphone was invented a long time ago. Similarly, the method of audio recording and transcription is now obsolescent because it involves a middleperson whose role could equally well be filled with a voice-recognition device which will translate documents straight on to the screen for approval and/or correction. Poor spelling can be corrected automatically by an appropriate piece of software. (Poor grammar is a different problem but one hopes the National Curriculum may solve this eventually!)

Equally, there are still people translating other people's thoughts and instructions onto computer. Perhaps some of them are obsolete too?

Both categories can be eliminated, even without voice-recognition equipment, by teaching more people keyboard skills and letting them deal direct with the machines. There are two obstacles – apart from the grammar. Managerial and supervisory vanity on the one hand and a vast pile of redundant middlepersons, with keyboard skills, on the other. But this, given the demographic time bomb, may instead be an opportunity – or several opportunities.

- The obvious one is that some of the typists, if tested and trained, may prove to suit jobs more closely associated with the IT function, thereby alleviating part of the predicted skills shortage.
- Managerial vanity is a barrier, but also an opportunity, in that if they are too resistant, perhaps they are not bright enough or well-balanced enough to be in the team? Perhaps one of the redundant secretaries would be better? Test and train, test and train.
- The third possibility is that managers may resist for valid reasons, because the middlepeople are doing other tasks – important ones – not visible in their job descriptions. This gives an opportunity to re-specify the real jobs and create new ones without the redundant content, thus filling them better, perhaps cheaper and certainly constructing more satisfying roles.
- Initially, this new philosophy may be misunderstood by potential employees to whom it is foreign, but it may open up a new pool of people at present under-recognized elsewhere, whose skills and maturity can be used better in your transformed organization. Married 'returners' come to mind: anyone who has dealt successfully with a young family has probably acquired many of the behavioural skills needed in a normal office or other workplace. Additionally, given the lack of higher educational opportunities for women twenty years ago and familial pressures before and since then, many women are more developable than their educational records suggest; they constitute hidden treasure. Find it. Use it.

Some of you may be practising much of this already, but a further review will probably identify gaps which can make you more profitable and more efficient.

Anyone who has dealt successfully with a
young family has probably acquired many of the behavioural
skills needed in the office

As an extra weapon to convince your colleagues, work out how many PCs and how much software you could buy for a secretary's annual salary . . . the trade-off is massive.

Once you have cut out the unnecessary middlepersons, you can address yourself to the next step – hiring the ideal candidates for what's left.

The Ideal Middle

'Middle what?' you may well ask. Middle anything is the general answer. We are used to the phrase 'middle management' which tends to obscure the fact that in most organizations there is a pecking order which puts the majority of employees in the middle of a sandwich, responsible to someone and directly or indirectly responsible for someone below them. It follows that there are factors common to most employees precisely because they are middlepersons. Anyone right at the top of the heap and those right at the bottom are different, but in the dominant middle we look for characteristics which will help people work well as part of the total team.

The practical and profitable benefits of avoiding the bad management characteristics outlined earlier should be self-evident but it may be helpful if we enlarge on the possibilities of getting all the middle people right. The list which follows is not exhaustive and it may be a useful exercise to add your own organization's shining examples – and the uncooperative ones you seek to avoid. As a general rule, departments staffed by the 'ideal middle' types are going to produce more work, more effectively with less staff and less hassle. They should also have less absenteeism and lower turnover:

- their error rate is lower, or non-existent
- they are happy to work direct onto computers, not via an intermediary (secretary or anyone else)
- they do not create demarcation disputes: if there is a long-term problem they will address it after they have solved the short-term crisis by helping out
- they do not waste time taking offence
- they are constructive: every problem is a chance for them to learn and/or train better rather than blame someone else
- they are communicative: they phone, or speak face-to-face rather than writing memos, although they will know when to confirm in writing; they will appreciate the merits of *short* fax messages at times when answering machines are unhelpful

- they will feel uncomfortable if they go home without earning today's revenues or meeting today's quota because they appreciate the basic truth that tomorrow is not going to be made extra long so that they can catch up
- they will belong to the 'puppy-dog' school of training, which operates on the basis that the person nearby at the time of an error has to advise the perpetrator *immediately* while the matter is still fresh: turning the problem into a 'federal case' is not effective.

This leads us naturally to the final important but unquantifiable bonus, the way middlepeople complain.

There are three variables. One is timing – instant or delayed. The second is the audience, which could be direct, ie the subject of the complaint, indirect – perhaps a relevant manager or supervisor – or irrelevant, ie anyone who cannot affect the matter. The third variable is, of course, the nature of the complaint, which could be constructive, wholly negative or something in between. Instant, direct and constructive comment is almost invariably the best bet. Even to a superior it can be couched as an innocent question and, if you have recruited correctly, the superior will be sensitive enough and apolitical enough to accept the message.

The alternative, the indirect and destructive complainant, is immensely damaging and wastes a lot of time. Interview questions about the way people have coped with recent problems in their peer groups need to be pursued to identify these types.

There is another category, often confused with the type immediately above, whom we can best describe as the 'social' complainant. These animals have, over many years (probably since childhood), lived in an atmosphere where they and others fill all conversational gaps with a dirge of low level complaint which they do not regard as requiring action, not least because they do not realize this is their conversational staple. Finding them at interview is not easy but if you deviate on to inconsequential trivia during the meeting it may be possible to elicit the background grumble, perhaps about BR, the weather or the English team . . .

Do not automatically reject them for a job but do recognize that you will have to vaccinate their colleagues against the effects. The same applies to some of the earlier characteristics. Do not reject absolutely, but do recognize what they may do to the balance of your team. Smooth out the worst excesses and the ideal middle will work wonders for you.

Keeping People

This may seem a trifle out of place in a book about recruitment, but it is important. Recruiting the people you've already got by retaining them is important. This is done on several levels:

- by spending money, time and effort so that they stay
- by not firing but recycling them
- by considering remedial action when they do resign and you don't want them to
- (slightly outside the definition) by recruiting those who used to work for you.

All these are bargains, for four reasons:

- you don't have to pay to recruit them
- they may be cheaper than replacements
- they already know the organization and the function
- you already know their merits, limitations and potential.

This has a bearing on other things: whenever you are considering the right pay increase for an existing employee, remember all of these factors. Equally, do remember the non-financial ways of encouraging them, like praise, interest, courteous behaviour, training, telling them where they are going (and telling them constructively where they are going wrong), listening to them etc.

If at any stage you do not consider an employee worth the effort this should tell you one of three things:

- you have recruited or used them wrongly
- you have not found out how good they could be
- if they genuinely are not good enough, don't put up with it, consider firing and rehiring.

Most terminations involve admitting management failure, so there is a temptation to do nothing, but this can demotivate others around the sub-standard performer. But always ask where else in the organization they would fit . . .

Do remember the non-financial ways of
encouraging them . . .

Losing people you should not have lost has two other disadvantages, in that they sometimes persuade colleagues to
follow them and, even if they do not, their departure unsettles
people who liked working with them and/or respected their
views.

There is another link between hiring people and keeping them
– the question of motivation. This is an abstract concept before
you have hired them, yet terribly important practically when
they are in your employ.

Most of the things you do to keep people are not declared to
the people you are going to hire, so you do not get credit for them
when advertising or at the point of making an offer. Two points
arise from this. First, it can be beneficial to stress in your written
brief to candidates those aspects of the 'keeping programme'
which can be codified and mention them again at interview –
some may even deserve mention in an offer letter. Second, if
some of the things cost a lot of money but don't help you to hire,
consider whether the mix between the solid benefits and the
unquantifiable should be changed or better presented.

Alas, you are going to get few brownie points for excellence in
management style – except to the extent that this is perceived at
interview – but there are other benefits which everyone within
the organization takes for granted and the outsider discounts
wholly or partially. Prospects come to mind; so does training.
But the most glaring example must be in the area of perfor-
mance-related rewards and, worse, the performance-unrelated
or partially related pay aspect. Specifically, let us consider
bonuses both from the hiring and keeping viewpoints.

Bonuses – Benefit or Burden?

To an employee, receiving a bonus is nice, particularly if he or she knows why it is being given (some companies don't say!). The short-term effect must be favourable, provided the employee doesn't feel cheated. (Did they expect more? Do they mistrust the way it is awarded? Did someone who doesn't deserve it get the same amount?)

They are a useful way of sharing out extra profit to key employees after the organization is certain it has earned the money. They should make key employees feel loved.

Unfortunately, bonus schemes are not primarily for the employees' benefit. In principle, they should exist for the employer's benefit, with the employees' welfare as a by-product! This confusion of purpose is widespread. This chapter, therefore, explores the value of staff bonuses to a typical industrial or commercial employer, with some attention to corrective action for schemes which turn out to be more of a burden than a benefit.

Objectives

The first point to clarify is the objective of a bonus scheme. Usually there are several objectives which typically include:

(a) reward for historic performance
(b) motivation in current and future work
(c) a way of keeping people
(d) a way of sharing profits (*not* synonymous with (a) above)
(e) a way of buying new people cheaply . . .

Formulae

The second variable is the scheme 'formula', by which the likely bonus is computed and guaranteed. For example:

(a) discretionary (ie unguaranteed) and random
(b) discretionary but linked to (i) perceived personal performance
(ii) corporate performance

(c) guaranteed, based on personal, quantifiable contribution of some kind
(d) guaranteed, based on corporate performance
(e) guaranteed, based on a mixture of corporate and personal performance.

The catch about these variables in relation to the stated objectives is that some types of bonus computation defeat or erode some of the objectives. Others fail in nearly all respects and create ill-will. These are sweeping statements, but they can be justified.

Discretionaries devalued

First of all, any bonus which is discretionary runs the risk of being misunderstood or under-appreciated. The employer certainly does not get value for money in terms of motivation, staff retention or buying power because the uncertainty devalues the bonus.

Worse, if the way the bonus is calculated is not clearly understood, the bonus scheme can actually create ill-will rather than goodwill.

Formulae fortify

Guaranteed bonuses are better, particularly if the formula is clearly linked to personal and achievable performance. However, they still suffer from credibility problems. Other things being equal, if new or existing employees are considering a base salary of £10,000 plus the possibility of earning an extra 20 per cent as a bonus, over twelve months away in the future, they will undoubtedly compare the package adversely against a salary of £12,000. They will probably compare it adversely against a base salary of £11,000 if they have doubts about the chances of earning the bonus. You will probably only get credit for just £10,000 in their mental calculation, so that the motivation you buy may not exceed £10,000 worth either!

The next problem is that if the bonus formula is linked to corporate performance, most individuals who don't manage their own profit centres cannot identify closely enough the connection between bonus and personal efforts. They may also feel offended that colleagues who are slacking are sharing equally in the pool – an instant demotivator! Mixing the corporate

If the way the bonus is calculated
is not easily understood . . .

performance element with a factor for the individual's achievement of personal objectives is a partial solution, if a fair assessment of the latter is possible. However, the discounting process remains and the employer does not get full value for money.

What is the solution? The objectives remain valid, but is the existing bonus scheme the right route to those objectives?

For a company with an existing bonus scheme the solution is probably easy. A fair salary policy with regular merit and cost-of-living reviews is probably best – making sure people understand on what objective criteria the merit element is assessed.

For the company with an existing scheme there are basically two choices – improvement or cessation. Improvement must depend on the local managing director's assessment of conditions and the availability of credible performance targets but, in my experience, few employees will be offended by a scheme which provides:

(a) that their company (or profit centre) has made significantly better real profits than in the previous period
(b) that a minority of the extra profit is allocated to a bonus pool, and
(c) that key employees share in that pool to an extent dictated by their *personal* performance on an understood formula.

Refinements can include the payment of last year's 'bonus' as an addition to the current year's base salary – quite useful in making the employee accept ever-increasing targets! A further refinement is to eliminate the maximum limit of bonus, if one exists. It is immensely damaging: not only does it demotivate people but, by definition, it selectively demotivates your *best* people.

Cessation remains an alternative. Why cease? There are very good grounds for it unless your existing scheme is near-perfect. (It will often be cleaner to 'buy out' a bad scheme rather than struggle to negotiate or impose improvements.) What are the grounds? Quite simply, unless you have a very good scheme you are (a) failing to achieve the objectives originally listed and (b) paying more than you need to for the limited results which can be obtained.

'Buying-out' a bad bonus scheme can be a very therapeutic exercise which can improve morale and motivation if done properly. It should ideally be combined with the annual salary review so that you can get the maximum impact – even on the worst peforming employees. For example, a classic 'buying-out' package could cover – let us say:

Cost of living element	9%
Merit element	10%
Bonus element	12%
	———
Total increment	31%
(and for non-merit earner	21%)

If this transition takes place at the time when the bonus would have been paid there is even a cash flow advantage! Further advantages include a likely short-term reduction in staff turn-over *and* the chance to buy new staff at more competitive rates, which increases the quality of people you can pluck from any given market. Conversely, if you don't convert – think of the people you are missing because 'jam tomorrow' doesn't equate to salary today.

All this may seem a bit one-sided, so we must recognize the virtues of bonus schemes! If you want employees who can help you make extra profit so that they can share in that profit, a well-constructed scheme is worthwhile and it enables you to defer payment until you know you can afford it. Provided you have no illusions about its value versus salary, the ranking order for rewarding people is probably:

WORST – low salary plus bad bonus scheme
GOOD   – higher salaries, no bonus
BEST   – market rate salaries, plus share of
         improved profits to key people only.

The things that turn a scheme from tolerable to bad are:

- uncertainty about calculation
- payment to the undeserving
- bonus unrelated to personal influence
- very late payment
- a ceiling on bonus potential
- low salaries 'balanced' by large bonus.

The catch is that you have to avoid *all* of them to get the maximum benefit! 'You pays your money and you takes your choice.'

136

THE FINAL MESSAGE

The Final Message

In spite of earlier dismissive comments in the 'Skills Explosion' chapter the author does recognize that some companies do, from time to time, have real skills shortages, or even unskilled gaps. These can be anywhere from IT to menial functions. Fortunately, the solution to these shortages is almost a reprise of the lessons of this book, in particular the earlier sections about making every stage of the recruitment process more reliable. Those earlier lessons made a case for doing everything 10 per cent better, to get more qualitative and practical benefits in comparison with whatever was your previous norm. With skills in short supply, this process moves up from being an option to a necessity. If you do not follow the rules as indicated earlier – and summarized below – you will remain short of people in a vital function.

The message for the skills deficiencies is, therefore, that of the book as a whole: successful recruitment flows from good, thorough practice, crossing the t's and dotting the i's at every point. This is to to say it is an unremitting grind. On the contrary, doing it well can be easier than some ways of doing it badly – or traditionally – depending on what the current practice is.

One other benefit must be that if you and your colleagues do it well, the successful recruitment will probably be earlier than usual. The results ought also to be of better quality and the benefits described in recent chapters should flow more obviously and in greater profusion! Read on, for the final round-up and, with luck and good behaviour, for a reliable solution in areas previously unreliable.

The Problems

Recruitment for a 'skills shortage' function is the same as *some* other recruitment, but different from the norm. These two sections will cover the differences and the similarities, the unique problems and the standard ones, plus the unique solutions, too.

First, the special problems, usually perceived as including:

- net shortage of adequately skilled and experienced people
- uncertainty of existing recruitment processes
- high cost of recruitment
- high staff turnover
- unavailability of permanent staff
- demographic factors which hit *young* recruits worst
- unusual personality profiles: poor communication skills!
- rapacious agencies!
- lack of training for today's needs.

We would add:

- unscientific definition of necessary candidate specification
- unnecessary discrimination
- lack of career development prospects and motivation.

Conventional Solutions

Next, the methodical, modular approach towards a solution. There are seven stages in the recruitment process:

- defining the nature of the vacancy
- agreeing the candidate specification and rewards
- planning the sourcing, including choice of 'agency' and media
- creating the marketing documents eg ad copy, job brief
- making it easy for good people to respond and to meet you
- assessing them
- making an offer and getting it accepted.

Being 10 per cent better at each of these can give you a cumulative 100 per cent boost in the quantity or quality of your results.

The earlier chapters cover several ways normal practice can be enhanced and the key item at each level, ie:

- better definition of the need for permanent/contract staff
- necessity to get rewards, person specification and job to fit
- adequate and early resourcing – no 'underkill' efforts. Obey the rules
- clear disclosure (no fudging)
- warm reply facility and interview arrangements
- tests (always better than interviews)
- discuss needs; don't just rely on salary. Remember the benefits menu.

And of course, make sure the induction programme enhances your efforts.

Other Solutions

Now, the more inventive solutions (lateral thinking may identify others):

- unless you have a time-machine you cannot train in 1986 for '89, but you can train *now* for '92.
- you can also test existing employees and switch or re-train them
- you can de-skill vacancies until they are more easily filled (internally or externally), perhaps with a little more training
- you can avoid discrimination more effectively than your competitors and have a wider choice (*all* employers are competitors in this context)
- attract volunteers
- make your problems your USP's
- borrow consultancy and agency techniques
- even without years of lead time, train and take a risk!
- don't take a huge space in one advertising medium . . . take half in two
- *negotiate* with agencies, in return for exclusivity
- make a good agency one arm of your people function
- get editorial coverage (thus volunteers!)
- keep people
- develop more inventive motivators/retention tools.

Finally, there is no absolute solution (without the time-machine) but you *can* create an environment in which the rewards treadmill becomes less important so you hire *better* people, quicker and more easily; people who are more relevant and loyal, better motivated and who stay longer.

APPENDIX

The International Dimension

This is about staffing the overseas subsidiary. It specifically deals with the principles and opportunities for a UK or European group seeking to establish or expand in another territory, but it is also applicable if you are trying to do it in the opposite direction. Practical details may vary but the principles remain valid.

There are two key principles. First, before planning the 'How', you need to be very sure about the 'Why'. Without a clear understanding of the objectives, all your planning may be flawed. Second, although the problems are appreciably greater than for local recruitment, the opportunities exceed the problems, not least because if you identify and solve the problems better than your competitors, you gain an automatic advantage over them. There is nothing quite so satisfying as seeing one of your own companies forging ahead quietly and without fuss while its major competitor (also a long-distance subsidiary) is behaving like a headless chicken because the parent company has either abdicated responsibility – without leaving anyone on site with a clear set of objectives and the authority to achieve them – or has interfered so much that local initiative is stifled and key staff demotivated to the extent that some leave and others are absent in spirit!

Actually, there is a third principle. It applies to most management matters but has no particular force in long-distance recruitment. Quite simply, you should be aiming for maximum results with minimum effort. Any departure from this principle implies horrendous waste of parent company time and travel costs.

At this point you may note that I am starting to make a case for delegation as a key factor in any exercise of this sort. Delegation is necessary on three levels:

(a) To get the ideal performance out of a distant subsidiary, you must delegate adequate authority to local management.

Don't create culture shock

(b) To get local management worthy of that authority you need to delegate their recruitment to someone who understands the local management market.

(c) To get support staff and labour who will live up to such management, that management must hire them and develop them without arbitrary input from head office. Few things are worse than giving 'total autonomy' in recruitment subject to the compulsory use of the local end of the parent's favourite UK recruiters. Not only does this breach the rule about delegation, it is also a recipe for mediocrity.

Unless the international quality control is very good, recruiters can differ substantially from office to office. There is no substitute for the sign so beloved of French restaurant proprietors and customers 'Le patron mange ici'. Performance from a recruitment outfit depends on the local boss. Choose accordingly.

Not only do you need to choose consultants more carefully, you also need to do your end of the task better when you work with and through them. For example:

- the briefing needs to be better
- the employment package must be more attractive
- the processing of candidates must be perfect
- legalities (eg visa, work permits) need special care
- spouses need review and reassurance
- induction must be foolproof.

I floated earlier the 'Why before How' rule; one area where this applies most crucially is the sourcing decision. No matter who is deciding, you or local management, this is still a complex multi-part operation. After asking 'Why appoint someone' you then have to ask 'Do we hire or promote?' If you promote, do you look for local or parent company candidates? If you hire, do you hire local nationals or parent nationals? Also, do you source by advertising, headhunting or via a consultancy which uses either or both. There is no one correct answer to this, except to stress that you *must* take advice. There are significant differences in management recruitment practices between the USA, the UK, the rest of Europe and elsewhere which mean that the best source in one country may be illegal or useless in another. For example, national advertising is virtually compulsory in Germany, works well in the UK, but is not really meaningful in the USA. 'Headhunting' is frowned on in some European countries, actionable at law but still very effective in the UK and a favourite source in the US. Take advice about the right method for your specific need. The answer may differ even within a country and from year to year.

The advice will cost money – eventually. However, the very high cost of getting a recruitment exercise wrong will be far greater. 'Getting it wrong' is expensive in two ways: the job is done badly or not at all for a while; the legal and moral costs of terminating an unsatisfactory employee are significant.

So far, I have carefully refrained from offering dogmatic opinions about what you should and should not do on the other side of the border. However, from all the references to the potential for failure, you will appreciate that past experience has left me with some strong views.

The message is simple. Minimize change. Particularly, *combine* the following:

- try not to move existing people from country to country
- don't hire into your UK company for a job elsewhere
- don't put people into territories they don't know
- don't create culture shock
- don't transfer people to unknown functions, products or corporate styles
- don't take spouses for granted.

All the horror stories that employers and headhunters will tell you relate to people's failure to adapt to change; spouses who couldn't come to terms with local shopping, customs or climate; managers who couldn't cope with learning a new company, language, job and product all at the same time; children who found the anti-kidnap regime too traumatic; existing management who found the imposition of an insensitive foreigner bad for internal relations; customers who virtually demanded that staff go native before they would deal with them; badly briefed newcomers who managed to offend host governments within days of arrival (with alcohol, dress, behaviour, opinions or even sex) – quite apart from offending local employees whose sensibilities and livelihood were threatened at the same time. It may seem extreme to quote these examples in the USA/UK/European context but we are very different nations – and there are

. . . the anti-kidnap regime